The Topper Book

Topper Sailing from Start to Finish

John Caig and Dave Cockerill

JOHN WILEY & SONS, LTD

Acknowledgements
The authors and publishers would like to
thanks Liz Mansell for taking the majority
of the photographs and Dave Cockerill and
Tim Davison for additional photographs.
Robert Spencer and Rachael Scarfe for sailing
in front of the camera and the Royal Lymington
Yacht Club for hosting the two day shoot.
Also, Nick Marshall for sailing for us in
Fournells, and Minorca Sailing for hosting
the one day shoot there.

Other Wiley Editorial Offices

John Wiley & Sons Inc., 111 River Street,
Hoboken, NJ 07030, USA

Jossey-Bass, 989 Market Street, San Francisco,
CA 94103-1471, USA

Wiley-VCH Verlag GmbH, Boschstr. 12,
D-69469 Weinheim, Germany

John Wiley & Sons Australia Ltd,
42 McDougall Street, Milton, Quennsland
4064, Australia

John Wiley & Sons (Asia) Pte Ltd,
2 Clementi Loop #02-01,
Jin Xing Distripark, Singapore 129809

John Wiley & Sons Canada Ltd,
22 Worcester Road, Etobicoke, Ontario,
Canada M9W 1L1

Wiley also publish its books in a variety of
electronic formats. Some content that
appears in print may not be available in
electronic books.

British Library Cataloguing in Publication Data:
A catalogue record for this book is available
from the British Library.

ISBN-10 1-904475-19-1
ISBN-13 978-1-904475-19-4

Designed and typeset by creativebyte
Printed in China through World Print
This book is printed on acid-free paper
responsibly manufactured from sustainable
forestry in which two trees are planted for each
one used for paper production.

Contents

Introduction

The Topper has a special place in sailing. Thousands of people learn the basic skills in Toppers every year.

But it's not just a beginner's boat as you will see by reading the later chapters of this book. Topper fleets are established at many sailing clubs, and the class association organises a programme of open meetings and championships for Topper enthusiasts.

Topper Sailing is for beginners and racers. We have organised the book in four parts:

Part 1 is for beginners and teaches sailors to rig and sail the boat.

We have also introduced the centre mainsheet here, because most sailors now use it. All the photos show the boat with gear in race configuration, but to keep things simple at this stage the race control lines are shown later in Masterclass 3.

Part 2 details the new small rig. This will be a boon for light sailors and for strong wind sailing for the less experienced.

Part 3 is an introduction to racing. If you get up to speed (see Part 1) and employ these tactics you should be able to win a club championship.

Part 4 is a masterclass with Dave Cockerill, National Topper Coach. Follow his advice, get out on the water, practise hard, and the sky's the limit…

1 The Topper story

The Topper's astonishing success as the first truly mass-produced racing dinghy is the result of a series of chance meetings and the exceptional vision and dedication of a few enterprising men.

In the early nineteen-seventies, John Dunhill was establishing a modest boat-building business and one day he chanced upon the moulds of a racy-looking little eleven-footer. Enquiries led him to the boat's designer, Ian Proctor, and he secured the right to build the boat – then named OD11 – in GRP (glass-reinforced plastic). John changed the name to Topper and the boat met with immediate success, coming out well on top in Yachting World's 'one of a kind' dingy rally in the summer of 1973.

At the London Boat Show, John Dunhill was approached by someone who told him that the company he represented – Rolinx Ltd, a subsidiary of ICI – had just developed a method of 'twinning' two enormous injection-moulding machines which would be capable of turning out Toppers in polypropylene at the rate of one every seven minutes; was he interested? Naturally he immediately responded to the long-term possibilities and, together with the directors of Rolinx, set about the task of raising the necessary quarter of a million pounds to commission

The Topper is built from two injection mouldings – one for the hull and one for the deck. This is a hull moulding lying alongside half of the die which was used to make it.

the injection-moulding tools. John had been most prudent in selling one of his GRP Toppers to a very senior executive in the Guinness Group and this man's enthusiasm for the boat – and later for the new production project – eventually led to Guinness taking over John Dunhill's company and providing 50 per cent of the initial tooling costs. The other half was put up by the National Research Development Corporation who clearly felt that the project was not only viable but of great importance to the prestige of Britain's world-leading plastics technology.

In 1977 the Topper received the Design Council award and Topper International Ltd (formerly J. V. Dunhill Boats Ltd) has now sold over 40,000 Toppers worldwide. Boats have been exported to over thirty countries and the dinghy has introduced thousands of people to an inexpensive but exciting new sport.

Copper braid is being inserted around the gunwale line of the deck moulding. The hull moulding is then clamped tightly on top. When electric current is passed through the braid, the two parts are permanently fused together.

2   Car Toppering

The Topper got its name in the first place because of the ease with which it could be transported on the roof of a car and this great mobility has certainly played a considerable part in the boat's worldwide success. The inverted boat presents a smooth, aerodynamic shape to the wind and neither speed nor fuel consumption is greatly affected during 'car toppering'. In fact, many caravan owners claim an improvement in consumption when towing because the Topper's shape guides the airflow around the bluff front of their 'vans.

In spite of the simplicity of the operation there are some important guidelines to follow if – like us – you drive many thousands of miles each year beneath a Topper. Position the two roof bars as far apart as possible on the car roof up to about a 4-foot maximum. It is quite acceptable for them to be much closer together than this as may be necessary if

you drive a coupe or rigid-topped sports car. Load the Topper upside down, bow forward and ensure that the front bar supports the side decks immediately behind the aft end of the foredeck. Ideally, the rear bar should support the side deck immediately ahead of the stern deck. Quick-release straps are by far the simplest means of securing the Topper and the least likely to come undone. If the bars are wide enough, you can lay the spars alongside the hull and take the straps right around the whole lot, which will greatly reduce loading time. Always tie the boat down to the bumpers (fenders) fore and aft. The bow painter can be used forward – this will stop the wind from lifting the boat – and the horse (traveller) can be used aft, where it will check any tendency for the boat to run forward in an emergency stop. A trolley can also be carried on top of the upside-down hull.

It is quite feasible to carry two Toppers on the roof of most cars but remember that the all-up weight will be 190 lb. The lower hull should be loaded *right way up*, bows forward. You will find that two Toppers fit together very snugly in this way – but do make sure that they are very well strapped down.

Part 1
Sailing the boat

3 Parts and rigging

The Topper is exceptionally simple and is supplied complete and ready to sail. The diagram opposite shows all the standard parts in place.

Earlier boats had a halyard to pull up the sail: rigging this is shown on page 15.

Race boats tend to have a centre mainsheet and chapter 4 shows how to fit this. They also have advanced control lines and these are detailed in Masterclass 3.

OK, let's put the boat together.

SAIL NUMBERS

Before you sail your new boat for the first time, it is most important to apply the self-adhesive numbers to the sail. The sail number is exclusive to the boat and corresponds to the serial number/sail number plate. These are inside the boat attached to the toestrap.

Follow the instructions carefully.

Standard Topper, sail numbers and national lettering

SAIL NUMBERS: (please note all measurements are minimums)
- Should be placed on both sides of the sail with the numbers on the starboard side being above the ones on the port side.
- They should be placed two panels below the Top Hat logo
- The height of the numbers should be 230mm.
- They may be pre-formed numbers or 'Digital Eights'.
- The preferred style of cutting 'Digital Eights' is shown below.
- There should be 45mm between each element of the complete number.
- The numbers should be in a contrasting colour to the white sailcloth

STARBOARD SIDE
- The upper edge of the numbers should be placed 45 mm from the upper seam of that panel
- They should start 45mm from the back of the sail.

PORT SIDE
- The upper edge of the port numbers should be 45mm below the starboard side numbers
- They should finish 45mm from the back of the sail.

GBR LETTERS
- Should be placed on both sides of the sail with the letters on the starboard side being above the ones on the port side.
- They should be placed in the panel beneath the Top Hat logo.
- The height of the letters should be 230mm.
- They should be pre-formed letters at least as clear as Helvetica
- There should be 45mm between each element of the complete letter.
- The letters should be the same colour as the sail numbers.

STARBOARD SIDE
- The upper edge of the letters should be placed 45 mm from the upper seam of that panel
- They should start 45mm from the back of the sail.

PORT SIDE
- The upper edge of the port letters should be 45mm below the ones on starboard.
- They should finish 45mm from the back of the sail.

Attaching numbers and letters.

In our experience the best way to stick the numbers down is to peel away the corner, line up the number and attach the corner. Pull away the backing paper slowly as you push onto the sail. Fiddly but it works!.

Topper 4.2, sail numbers and national lettering.

This is the same as for the Standard Topper except the GBR letters should be placed in the panel beneath the sail numbers.

1 Hull
2 Daggerboard (prevents sideways drift)

Ropes
3 Halyard (if fitted – keeps sail up)
4 Kicking strap or vang (prevents boom rising)
5 Downhaul (tightens front edge of sail)
6 Mainsheet (trims sail). Centre mainsheet
   also available
7 Outhaul (tightens foot of sail)
8 Clew tie-down (attaches corner of
   sail to boom)
9 Horse (traveller)
10 Painter (for tying up or towing)

Spars
11 Two-part mast
12 Boom

For steering
13 Rudder
14 Rudder stock
15 Tiller
16 Tiller extension (lets you
   steer when sitting out)

Sail
17 Sail
18 Sail numbers
19 Topper insignia

Other fittings
20 Toestraps
   (hiking straps)
21 Self bailer
   (to remove water)
22 Masthead crane
23 Mast gate

25000

When you have unpacked everythig, lay
out the various control lines on the foredeck
and identify them:

A Halyard loop
B Kicking strap (vang)
C Downhaul
D Mainsheet system
E Bow painter
F Outhaul
G Rope horse (traveller)
H Daggerboard elastic (shockcord)
I Toestrap elastic (shockcord)

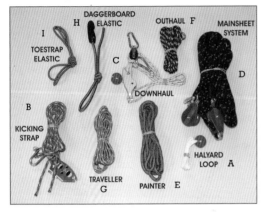

Halyard Loop
Please note that the upper mast has been turned
so the crane faces forward.
1. Feed the halyard loop up through the front
hole in the mast crane.
2. Down the back hole.
3. Through the eyelets of the sail and
back up the back hole (which might
need enlarging slightly with a drill).
4. Loop the end over the bobble at
the front.
5. So that it tucks under the bobble.
6 & 7. Pull the rope both sides of
the crane and up into the groove
on top of the mast-crane. This will
tension the rope and so lift the sail.

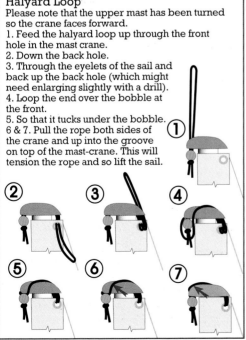

1. Slot the two mast sections
together, making sure that the slots in the
upper section have engaged properly with
the rivets in the lower section (photo A).

2. Sleeving the sail: halyard loop method
a. Unfold the sail and lay it on the ground
   with the bottom edge of the luff sleeve
   near the top of the mast.
b. Insert the mast into the luff sleeve (photo
   B) and pull the sail down the mast (photo
   C). If it is at all windy, keep your back to
   the wind!
c. Continue until the whole sail is sleeved
   and the masthead has appeared through
   the top of the sail.
d. Use the halyard loop to attach the sail to
   the top of the mast as shown in the panel.

Sleeving the sail: halyard method

Pass one end of the main halyard through the masthead crane and tie a knot. Pull the halyard tight and cleat off on the halyard cleat. This will hold the mast together while you pull the sail onto it.

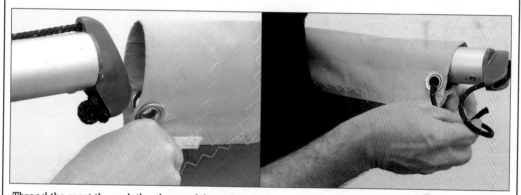

Thread the mast through the sleeve of the sail and when the mast appears through at the top, undo both ends and tie the halyard to the top of the sail. If you're using a burgee, fit it into the top of the mast now. Go back to the foot of the mast, pull the halyard very tight and re-fasten it to the cleat at the front of the mast. Coil the rope and tuck it under itself, above the cleat.

Attach the downhaul to the tack cringle (above) and make off on the cleat (right).

If it is at all windy it is advisable to roll up the sail around the mast before stepping.

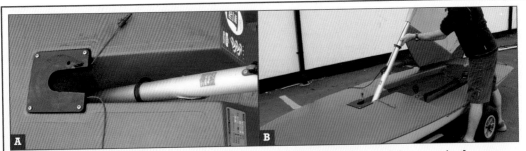

3. Stepping the mast

A. Point the boat into the wind. Support the mast at a 45 degree angle and engage the base of the mast in the cup under the mast gate.

B. Walk the mast forward into an upright

4. Rigging the outhaul

Take the outhaul line through the boom-end fitting and outhaul hook and back through the boom-end eye. Finish with a figure of eight knot (photos F-K).

Take the other end of the outhaul line through the kicker fitting and cleat, and tie a loop (photos L-M). Note: the outhaul is long, to allow for reefing (see chapter 6).

Finally, push the boom crutch onto the mast above the collar, making sure that the downhaul is outside the crutch (photo N).

Setting the outhaul

Tension the outhaul initially to give a slight curve in the foot of the sail. The maximum draft should not exceed three to four inches between sail and boom at the midpoint.

position, ensuring that the collar is underneath the mast gate.

C. Pull the cord to close the gate.

D. Tie a loop in the rope as a backup in case the toggle comes out.

E. Push the toggle in firmly to lock the gate.

5. Rigging the sheet horse (traveller) and mainsheet

Tie a bowline (20 mm) in one end of the rope that will become the sheet horse (traveller). Thread the tail through the two fairleads, back through the bowline loop and down through the horse clam cleat. Tie a figure of eight knot in the end of the sheet horse (photo O).

Shackle the lower mainsheet block to the sheet horse (traveller) (photo P) and shackle the upper mainsheet block to the boom (photo Q).Tie a knot in the free end of the mainsheet (photo R). Photo S shows the complete system. If the sail was rolled, unroll it. Attach the clew to the outhaul clip and to the clew ring (photos T, U and V).

6. Rigging the kicking strap (vang) and downhaul

1. Attach the kicking strap (vang) to the mast with the clevis pin and split ring. Attach the other end by clipping the hook onto the metal ring beneath the boom.

2. Clip the downhaul hook through both tack cringles on the sail. Clip the other end to the ring on the aft face of the mast.

On older boats the kicker looks like these two photos (below).

 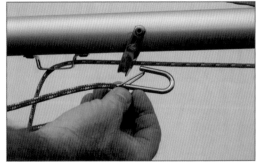

Setting the kicking strap (vang)

The 'normal' tension is achieved by first tightening the mainsheet and then taking up the slack on the kicking strap so it is just tight. This will give the correct tension on the boom when reaching or running. Since the mainsheet's tension will be varied for different wind conditions the kicking strap should be varied accordingly. It is not easy to adjust the standard kicking strap while actually reaching or running except in very light winds. The race kicking strap is easily adjusted anytime.

7. Rudder, toestrap and daggerboard.

1. Attach the tiller to the rudder balde with the bolt provided.

2. With the blade in the raised position, pass the tiller under the rope traveller and lower the rudder onto the transom fitting (photo A). Ensure that it is completely home and that the spring retaining clip has engaged to prevent the rudder becoming detached in a capsize (photo B). The blade is lowered by lifting and pushing back on the tiller. Lower the tiller again when the blade is down (i.e. vertical).

3. With the shockcord provided, tie the toestraps tightly towards each other at the aft end – you can stow the daggerboard behind one of the outer toestraps when it's not in use (photo C).

4. The daggerboard is kept in the desired position by the tension in the shockcord, which creates a forward wedging action in the daggerboard housing. Loop the shock-cord round the mast between the webbing strap and mastgate and clip it onto itself with the hook (photo D). Pass the free end of the shockcord through the top of the hole in the daggerboard rim (photo E). Adjust the tension to suit, then tie a retaining knot (photo F).

You may be surprised to discover that the daggerboard floats. But the rudder assembly – due to its cast-alloy stock – does not! So be careful when shipping or unshipping the rudder when afloat.

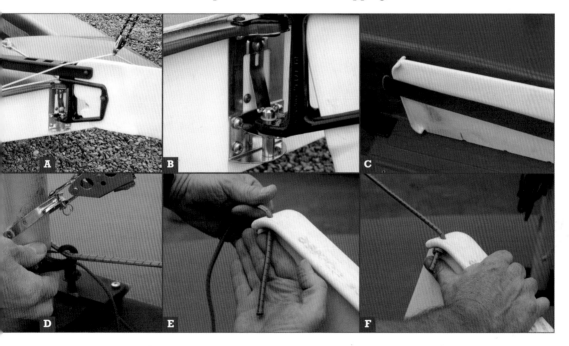

Going further

The Topper is easier to sail with better control lines and certainly if you want to race, the standard boat should be upgraded. It is fine as a beach boat but if you want to get into the the top 90% of the fleet you need race controls and you will need to know how to use them properly.

The standard traveller rope is replaced by non-stretch, with a better cleat. The kicking strap, outhaul and downhaul have increased purchases. Details are in Masterclass 3. The centre mainsheet is discussed in chapter 4.

4 The centre mainsheet

For years the aft sheeting system was the only one allowed. Now we can lead the mainsheet forward to the top of the daggerboard case. This has proved a great success and the photos in this book show the centre mainsheet.

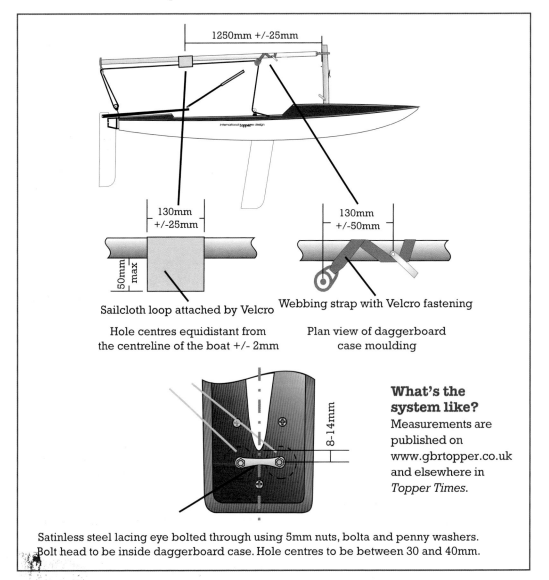

1250mm +/-25mm

130mm +/-25mm

50mm max

Sailcloth loop attached by Velcro

Hole centres equidistant from the centreline of the boat +/- 2mm

130mm +/-50mm

Webbing strap with Velcro fastening

Plan view of daggerboard case moulding

8-14mm

What's the system like?
Measurements are published on www.gbrtopper.co.uk and elsewhere in *Topper Times*.

Satinless steel lacing eye bolted through using 5mm nuts, bolta and penny washers. Bolt head to be inside daggerboard case. Hole centres to be between 30 and 40mm.

Strapping the forward block to the boom.

The aft sheeting system, with a traveller across the transom, was retained with the rope being led along the boom and down to a ratchet block on the top of the dagger-board case moulding. The attachment at this point is by bolting through from the inside of the moulding, a straightforward job. A sailcloth loop is added on the boom to prevent the rope dangling, when slack, and lassoing the poor sailor!

Webbing straps and Velcro are used to attach the additional block to the boom, as there seemed no point in weakening the boom by drilling extra holes.

Why has the centre mainsheet become the preferred arrangement for racing?

- Transferring to and from other boats is less challenging.
- In strong winds the aft sheeting pulled you to the back of the boat. The way to prevent this was to twist forward, which was both uncomfortable and tiring. Sailors can now hike straight out.
- By the same token, sailors can pivot backwards more effectively when beating through waves.
- Pulling in the mainsheet across your body was less efficient than pulling towards you. The sheet loads on a

Topper were a challenge for younger sailors. Less strength is required with the centre sheeting.
- Gybing and tacking facing forward allow the sailor to see where they are going. After all we don't corner a car while looking out of the back window!

HOW IS IT DONE?

The boom

The boom end block
This is hung in the same way as the original. The present block needs changing for a becket version and a shorter rigging link needs to be used between the boom end fitting and the block. This keeps the mainsheet closer to the boom.

The forward boom block
This is attached to the boom with a webbing strop (or rope) by weaving it through the kicker take off point. The ends of the webbing are joined with Velcro

The traveller block
The current ratchet block is changed for a non-becket block. Use a rounded (forged) shackle so the traveller doesn't get worn.

7/2063005

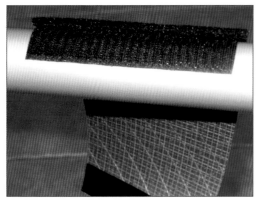

The boom loop.

The boom loop

The loop, to prevent the sailor being lassoed, is attached to the boom with self-adhesive Velcro. Most dealers will supply the material with Velcro sewn on.

The hull fittings

Two holes need drilling in the hull. Your dealer should include a template with the kit. The process is:

- Unscrew the hull plate and remove the bladders.
- Mark out and drill the two holes right through the hull from above.
- Put penny washers on the bolts and push the bolts through from the inside.
- Bolt on the deck eye. It is best to use nyloc nuts.
- Shackle on the ratchet block, and away you go!

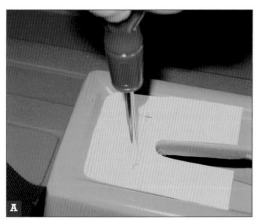

Marking out the template.

Removing the hullplate.

Pulling out the bladders.

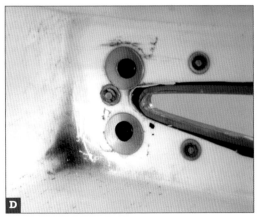

View inside the moulding.

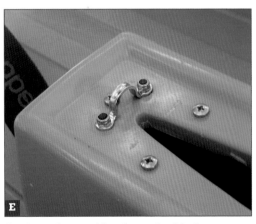

Deck eye for attaching the ratchet block.

5 Sailing theory

WIND

WIND

Take a careful look at these photographs. You will see that:

- The helmsman sits on the windward side of the boat (to balance the wind pushing on the sail).
- The helmsman always holds the tiller in his aft (back) hand. He steers with the tiller.
- The helmsman always holds the mainsheet in his forward (front) hand. The mainsheet adjusts the angle of the sail to the centreline of the boat.

How does the boat sail?
Wind is the Topper's driving force. The wind flows over the windward side of the

sail (causing pressure) and round the leeward side (causing suction). The resulting force on the sail is in the direction of arrow A, i.e. it is at right angles to the sail.

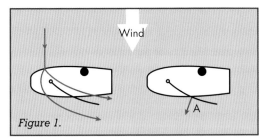

Figure 1.

The force pushes the boat forwards and sideways. The forwards push is welcome! The sideways push is counteracted by water pressure on the daggerboard (figure 2).

The helmsman's weight counteracts the heeling (capsizing) effect. The further he leans out, the more leverage he gets.

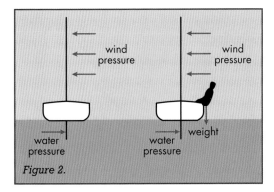

Figure 2.

If the sail is pulled in, force A will be almost at right angles to the boat: the sideways force is maximum, and the daggerboard needs to be pushed right down to counteract it (figure 3). If the sail is let out, force A points forwards: there is no sideways force, so the daggerboard can be pulled up.

How can I steer?

When a boat is sailing straight, the water flows past the rudder undisturbed. When the rudder is turned, the water is deflected. The water hitting the rudder pushes it, and the

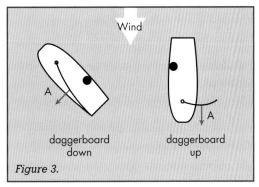

Figure 3.

back of the boat, in direction B (figure 4). The bow turns to the left.

In short, pulling the tiller towards you turns the bow away from you, and vice versa.

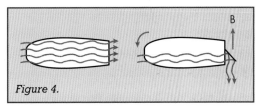

Figure 4.

How can I stop?

It is the wind in the sail that makes a boat go forward. To stop it, take the wind out of the sail either by letting go of the mainsheet, or by altering course towards the wind (figure 5).

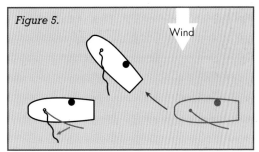

Figure 5.

How can I tell which way the wind is blowing?

Everything in sailing is related to the wind direction. You can tell which way it's blowing by the feel of it on your cheek, by the wave direction or by using a burgee. Remember, the burgee points to where the wind is going.

POINTS OF SAIILING

Look at figure 7 on the opposite page. There are three points of sailing:

1 *Reaching* – the boat sails across the wind (see photo A)
2 *Beating* – the boat sails towards the wind (photo B)
3 *Running* – the boat sails with the wind from behind (photo C)

Reaching

The boat in photo A is reaching. It is sailing at right angles to the wind, which is blowing from behind the helmsman's back. The sail is about halfway out and the daggerboard halfway up.

Beating

If you want to change course towards the wind, you mush push the daggerboard down and pull in the sail as you turn. You can go on turning towards the wind until the sail is pulled right in. Then you are *beating* (photo B).

If you try to turn further towards the wind, you enter the 'no go area'. The sail flaps and the boat stops.

To get from A to B (figure 4), the only way is to beat in a zigzag fashion.

At the end of each 'zig' the boat turns through an angle of 90°. This is called a tack. The boat turns 'through' the wind – the sail blows across to the other side and the helmsman must shift his weight across the boat to balance it.

Running

From a reach, you may want to change course away from the wind. Pull up the daggerboard (not more than three-quarters up) and let out the sail as you turn. You can go on turning until the wind is coming form behind the boat. Then you are *running* (photo C). If you turn more the boat will gybe. That is, you will find the wind is suddenly blowing from the opposite side of the sail which then flies across to the other side of the boat very quickly. Be on your guard against this happening inadvertently.

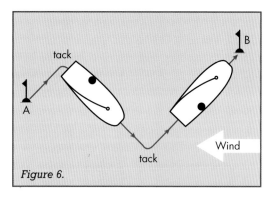

Figure 6.

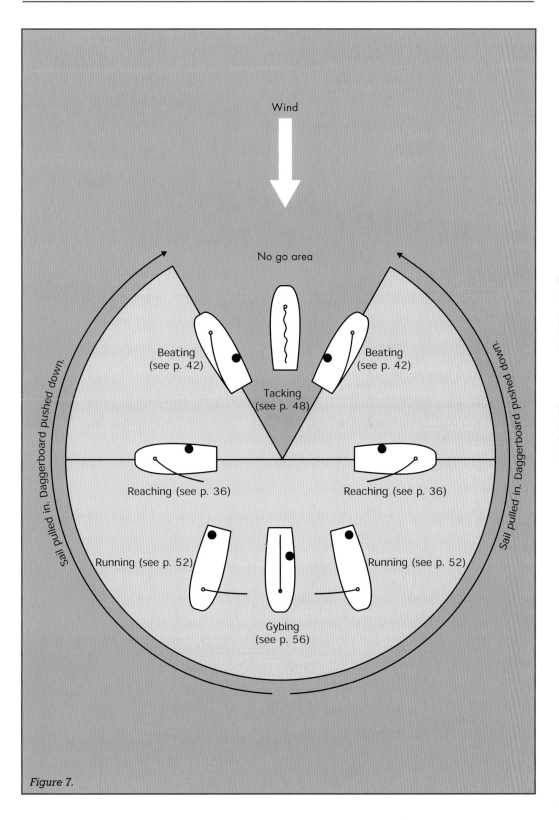

Wind

No go area

Beating
(see p. 42)

Beating
(see p. 42)

Tacking
(see p. 48)

Sail pulled in. Daggerboard pushed down.

Sail pulled in. Daggerboard pushed down.

Reaching (see p. 36)

Reaching (see p. 36)

Running (see p. 52)

Running (see p. 52)

Gybing
(see p. 56)

Figure 7.

6 Reefing

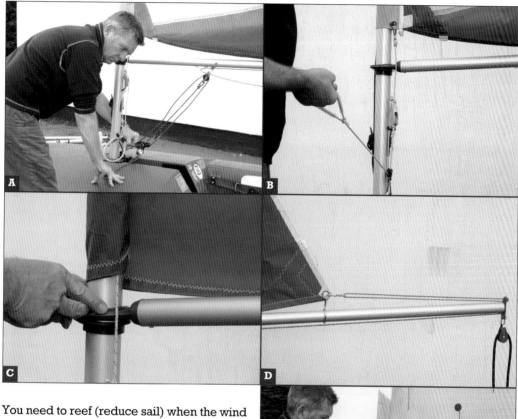

You need to reef (reduce sail) when the wind is strong. If you think you will have difficulty in holding the boat up on the beat, or will capsize on the run, then reef. (Alternatively, invest in a small sail.)

The Topper has been carefully designed so that you can reef out at sea. However, for the first few times you will find it easier to work on land or at the jetty. Here are the steps you take.

1 Start with the sail rigged normally.

2 Take off the kicker at the mast end only (photo A).

3 Pull on lots of downhaul, to prevent the sail twisting when you have rolled it up (photo B).

4 Ease out the outhaul. Rotate the mast at least twice, making sure the halyard moves properly inside the gooseneck. If the downhaul is on the port side, rotate the mast anticlockwise, viewed from above (photo C).

5 Tighten the outhaul (photo D) and re-rig the kicking strap (vang) (photo E).

6 If the wind drops, take out the reefs: let the sail flap, unclip the kicking strap, unroll the sail and tighten the outhaul. Re-rig the kicking strap, pull in the mainsheet and you're away again!

7 Launching

A

Always rig the boat before launching; if you are sailing from a jetty the sail can be rolled up completely around the mast and unfurled just before you set off.

Put the rudder on but pull it right up. Launch the boat on its trolley, keeping it pointing into the wind all the time. Once the boat is floating you can slide out the trolley and pass it to a friend (photo A).

Always use the trolley to launch and retrieve your Topper – without it you are very likely to scratch the bottom of the boat.

Launching from a beach with an offshore wind

This is the easiest wind direction to launch in (figure 1). Push a little rudder and dagger-board down (photo B). Turn the boat slightly

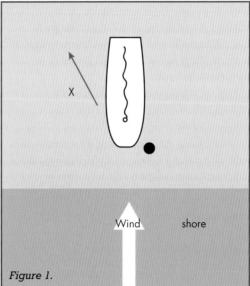

X

Wind   shore

Figure 1.

B

C

away from the wind, jump in, pull in the mainsheet slightly and sail slowly into deeper water (direction X) (photos C and D), where you can put the rudder and board right down. Don't try to sail hard or allow the boat to heel excessively with the rudder up or you may damage the rudder or it's fastenings.

D

Launching with an onshore wind

This is more difficult since you will need to beat in shallow water to get away from the shore. Launch with the rudder up and the boat pointing into the wind. Choose the tack which takes you away from the shore at the greatest angle; push off, getting as much daggerboard down as the depth will allow as early as possible (figure 2).

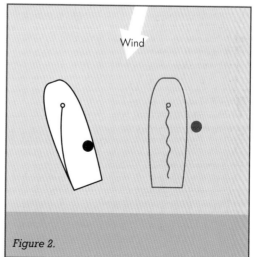

Figure 2.

8   A first sail

WIND

A **B** **C**

A dry run ashore

Before setting sail for the first time it is a very good idea to rig the boat completely, place it on a soft surface such as grass, and practise steering (with rudder and daggerboard up, of course!), adjusting the mainsheet, tacking, etc. This will give you much more confidence when you finally go afloat.

First time afloat

Try to choose a day with a gentle breeze for your first sail. Wind is measured either on the Beaufort scale or in knots. Force 4 (11 knots) or above would be unsuitable.

A reservoir, river or estuary is a good place to learn to sail. If you are learning on the open sea try to avoid an offshore wind (wind blowing from shore to sea) – you may get blown a long way from the shore. Always wear a lifejacket, and stay with the boat whatever happens.

Rig the boat as described in chapter 3. Reef (chapter 6) or use a smaller sail if there's much wind. Get a friend to help you launch (chapter 7); they should hold the boat for you while you lower the rudder and put in the daggerboard – then one good push and you're away.

As soon as you can, get sailing on a reach (photo A) with the wind blowing at right angles to the boat. The daggerboard should be about half up and the sail about half out. Sit on the side opposite the sail. Practise adjusting the mainsheet and steering. Try to get the 'feel' of the boat, particularly using your weight to balance the wind in the sail. (Reaching is discussed in chapter 9.)

Eventually you will need to tack (turn round) and reach back again (photos B and C). Tacking is described in chapter 11. Try to tack smoothly, changing sides and swapping hands on the tiller and mainsheet as you do so.

If the boat stops during a tack, keep the tiller central and wait until the boat starts to drift backwards. Eventually it will turn to one side and you'll be able to get

sailing again (photos D, E and F).

Reach back and forth until you feel confident. Try picking an object and sailing straight towards it, adjusting the mainsheet so the sail is as far out as possible without flapping. If a gust comes, let out the mainsheet (photos G and H). Try to keep the boat moving.

Next try picking objects slightly closer to or slightly further away from the wind. Try sailing towards them, adjusting the mainsheet.

When you have had enough, head for the shore, taking care to pull up the daggerboard and rudder in good time. Just before stepping out of the boat ease the sheet right out and head into the wind – making sure the water is shallow! Landing is discussed in more detail in chapter 16.

If you get stuck halfway through a tack, wait until the boat drifts backwards (you can help it by pushing out the boom). Eventually it will turn. Then pull in the mainsheet and sail off again.

G

In a gust, let out the mainsheet.

H

The boat will stop heeling immediately!

Sailing two up

Although the class rules, at the time of writing, do not permit more than one person in the boat when racing, two people can have great fun in a Topper.

To stop the stern dragging in the water and slowing the boat down, it is important that both helm and crew sit as far forward as possible. This also helps when tacking – so long as the crew at the front is careful to duck under the kicking strap (vang) when crossing the boat. When running or reaching in light winds, the boat is easily balanced by one person sitting on each sidedeck.

The next steps

When you feel happy reaching and tacking, you are ready to try the other points of sailing (see pages 26 and 27). You should still reef if there is much wind (more than Force 3).

One good way to practise is to sail round a square 'course' (Figure 1).

From a reach, gradually turn away from the wind, letting out the sail and pulling the daggerboard three-quarters up. You are now running. After a while, pull the tiller towards you, and gybe. Now reach the other way, with the daggerboard half down and the mainsheet half out. Next, push the daggerboard right down and turn towards the wind, pulling in your sail. You are beating. Tack, and beat the other way. When you are far enough into the wind turn off onto a reach, letting the sail out and pulling the daggerboard half up. Try several laps.

Remember:

- Sit on the windward side.
- Keep the mainsheet in your front hand, the tiller in your back hand.
- If you get out of control, let go of the mainsheet.

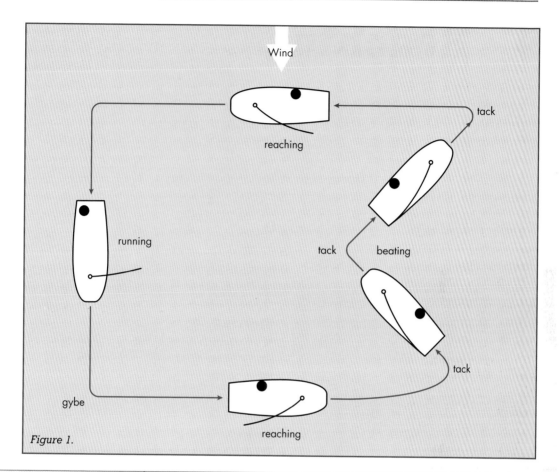

Wind

reaching

tack

running

tack   beating

tack

gybe

reaching

Figure 1.

If you need to pull in lots of mainsheet, use your sheet hand, then your tiller hand (still holding the tiller extension). Repeat as often as is necessary.

9 Reaching

Reaching is the easiest point of sailing and in a breeze the fastest and most exciting.

What is reaching?

The Toppers in Figure 1 are reaching. Their courses are roughly at right angles to the wind.

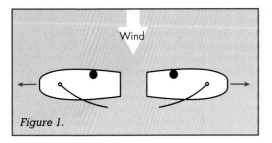

Figure 1.

Adjusting the sail

The secret of reaching is sail trim. Always try to let the sail out as far as it will go without flapping.

Although the wind may vary in direction from moment to moment it is always possible when reaching to continue to steer in the direction that you wish to go. However, to maintain the fastest speed you must continually adjust the position of the boom, and hence the sail, via the mainsheet. Every few seconds, ease the mainsheet out until the front edge of the sail (luff) begins to lift and then pull it in until this flapping stops (figure 2).

When you alter course you will have to adjust the sail angle accordingly. As you luff up (point your boat nearer the wind direction) pull the sail in, and as you bear away (point your boat away from the wind direction) ease the sail out.

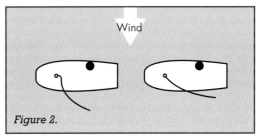

Figure 2.

Steering

Try to keep a reasonably straight course. Everything being equal the shortest distance between two points is a straight line! Remember, every time you move the rudder you slow the boat very slightly.

Trim

The trim of the boat (the angle at which the hull sits in the water) is affected by the wind strength, the boat's speed and, above all, the location of your body weight. Sit forward in light winds to reduce the amount of hull skin in the water (and so reduce skin friction). Move aft in strong winds to lift the bow and help the boat skim over the water – this is planing. Do not allow the boat to heel excessively since this will encourage it to turn into the wind. You will have to take corrective action with the rudder (with associated braking) to maintain a straight course – this is called 'weather helm'.

Bear away each time a wave picks up the boat, and try to surf on the wave.

Daggerboard

The daggerboard should not be fully down when reaching. The less you have down the less will be the drag resistance, and therefore the faster you will go. Half board is a good starting point, more being needed as you luff closer to the wind, to stop you slipping sideways.

Sail controls

The sail should be set with a good curve or belly in it. At least 4 inches between the foot of the sail and the boom at its midpoint is desirable. The kicking strap (vang) should be normal but the outhaul and downhaul should both be eased considerably.

Gusts

When overpowered (i.e. when the wind is too strong for you to hold the boat flat without letting the sail flap) ease the mainsheet and bear away from the wind. Sheet in again and luff back to your normal course when the gust has passed.

Going faster

Fast reaching helps win races. Here are some important points.

- Adjust the mainsheet all the time.
- Continually let out the sail until it flaps at the front, then pull it in until it just stops.
- Keep the boat upright all the time; sit out hard rather than ease the mainsheet to spill wind. Move back in the gusts and forward again as the wind drops.

- Steer a straight course (except during gusts).
- Look over your shoulder to see if a gust is coming – the water looks darker where a gust is travelling across it. When the gust hits bear away and sit out harder and ease the mainsheet a little. As the gust passes, luff up, sit inboard and pull the mainsheet in again.
- Pull up the daggerboard one notch (on the back of the board). Sit with your

Look at the telltales on the sail to help you trim it (left). Excellent reaching technique (centre and right).

knees against the daggerboard case.
- Set the downhaul completely slack.
  Set the outhaul so there is a hand-width between the foot of the sail and the boom. Set the kicker so that the leech just opens when a gust comes through.

The photos show good reaching style. The skippers are using their weight to keep the boat absolutely level. Their attention is on the front part of the sail (as well as where they're going!) and they continually adjust the mainsheet. Because the boat is level, they can steer gently and easily. The kicking strap (vang) is tight, but the other controls are loose. The sail has a good curve in it for maximum power.

REACHING IN LIGHT WINDS

Reaching in light winds, like all light wind sailing, needs patience. Keep very still so you don't shake the shape out of the sail. If you need to move, do so slowly.

Trim

Sit forward to lift the stern out of the water and reduce the wetted area of the hull, and hence skin friction.

Heel the boat to windward if there is sufficient wind to fill the sail, holding the boom out with your forward hand. This reduces the wetted area still further and neutralises the weather helm normally created by the sail effort turning the boat into the wind.

In extremely light airs sit to leeward on the foredeck just behind the mast. This reduces the wetted area to a minimum and helps hold some shape in the sail.

Gusts

When a puff arrives, bear away to try and

Good light wind technique.

stay with it as long as possible. Above all
this will take you below the direct line to the
next mark and enable you to luff up in the
lulls, thereby increasing your speed by up
to 50 per cent in certain conditions.

Sail controls
The downhaul and outhaul should be loose.
The kicking strap (vang) should be slightly
looser than normal. Aim for a lot of curve in
the sail (see photos).

Steering
Move the tiller as infrequently and slowly
as possible.

Going faster on a light reach
Use the rudder as little as possible.
Set the kicking strap so the leach opens
occasionally. Sit as far forward as you
can without hitting the foredeck. The
outhaul is loose to give a fairly deep sail.
The downhaul is right off, but if the wind
dies more, pull the outhaul out to flatten
the sail. Then also put on a bit more kicker
to take the slack out of the sail. Notice the
boat is heeled slightly to windward to
balance the rudder.

REACHING IN STRONG WINDS
Reaching in a Topper is extremely exhilar-
ating in a blow. You are close to the water so
the sensation of speed is remarkable.

Trim
Sit back enough to bring the bow up and
promote a good planing angle.You will
be at the back of the daggerboard case.
In very strong winds hike from the middle of
the side deck (this is the widest part of the
boat so your weight gives the maximum
righting effect here).

Gusts
When overpowered (i.e. when the wind is too
strong for you to hold the boat flat without
letting the sail flap) bear away from the wind,
luffing back above the direct course only
when the gust passes. Never let the sail flap
more than is necessary to keep the boat flat
and always sit out as far as possible. In this
way you will keep the maximum power on.

Sail controls
In strong winds the kicking strap (vang),
outhaul and downhaul should be set up
quite tightly and not touched (in any case
you would find it difficult to make adjust-
ments in these conditions, unless you have
race controls).

Daggerboard
With the daggerboard half up there will be
adequate board in the water to offset the
sideways forces, yet not enough to create
excessive drag.

REACHING – SOME COMMON MISTAKES

The kicking strap is too tight...   *correct...*   *and too loose (note the boom goes up in the air and power is lost).*

The sail is too far out. Pull in the mainsheet until the front edge of the sail just stops flapping.

The sail is too far in, which is heeling the boat.

Don't let the boat heel. Note the tiller pulled to windward to keep the boat straight.

That's better! Use your weight to bring the boat level. Note the straight rudder.

10 Beating

Beating to windward in a Topper is particularly satisfying. The boat is so lively and responsive that it's a joy to sail in virtually all conditions.

What is beating?

A boat cannot sail straight from X to Y (figure 1). The sail will flap, and the boat will be blown backwards. The only way is to beat – to sail a zigzag course at an angle of about 45° to the wind.

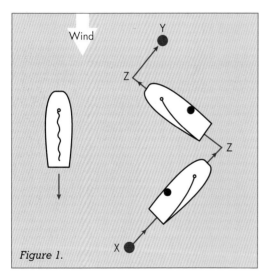

Figure 1.

Steering

To beat, pull in the mainsheet pretty much as hard as you can until the mainsheet block and boom end block nearly touch; sit out, and steer as close to the wind as you can. The course is a compromise: if you steer too close to the wind you slow down, even though you are pointing closer to Y. If you steer too far from the wind, you go faster, but are pointing well away from Y (figure 2).

The simplest check on your course is to watch the front of the sail. Turn towards the wind until the sail begins to flap, then turn back until it just stops flapping. You are now on course. Repeat this every few seconds – both to check your course, and because the wind constantly changes its direction.

At points Z the boat tacks through about 90°. Tacking is discussed in chapter 11.

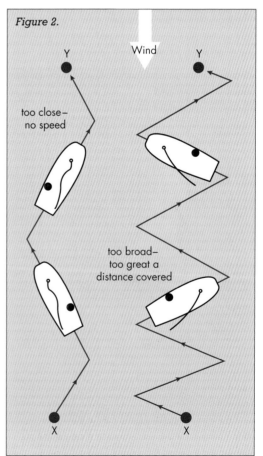

Figure 2.

Adjusting the horse (traveller)

Normally the horse should be pulled in tight – very tight in strong winds and only eased very slightly in light winds.

Adjusting the sail

When beating in medium or light winds there is no need to adjust the mainsheet. Keep it pulled in, and concentrate on using the tiller to keep the boat at the proper angle to the wind.

The tension on the mainsheet is important. In medium winds, pull it in until the main-sheet and boom end blocks are nearly touching. In light and in very strong winds, you will need to let the mainsheet out a little.

Trim

Sit forward, right up against the bulkhead, then either sit out or slide down to leeward with knees bent depending on the wind strength – you should aim for a constant 10° heel to reduce skin friction. Don't allow the boat to heel further than this in strong winds.

Daggerboard

The daggerboard should be right down when beating, except in strong winds.

Gusts

You should learn to spot a gust approaching by the dark pattern (tiny wavelets) that it creates on the water. As it arrives luff up slightly and sit out hard – it is much easier to prevent the boat from heeling than to recover when it does!

Windshifts

The wind constantly alters in direction. However, some changes are larger and /or last longer. These are windshifts, and it is vital you spot them and react to them when racing. Windshifts are discussed in Part 3.

Sail controls

The sail should be flattened off when beating

Pull in the mainsheet to correct beating position (about 10 cm between the blocks). Then tighten the kicking strap (vang) – and pull it a bit more!

Then, when you ease the mainsheet in a gust, the boom goes out, not up.

to reduce heeling forces and drag. The stronger the wind the flatter it needs to be.

The downhaul (Cunningham) should be set just to remove the horizontal creases in light winds, and tightened progressively as the wind gets stronger. This tension affects the whole of the sail and pulls the draft (maximum curve) of the sail forward, reducing drag.

The outhaul should normally be set to give 100-150 mm of draft in the middle of the foot in light and medium winds. It needs to be tensioned as the wind increases until it is curling the foot upwards in over-powering conditions. This control affects the draft in the lower part of the sail only.

The kicking strap (vang) tension is quite critical when beating. It needs to be slightly less tight when sailing over waves

in light weather but quite tight in smooth water, particularly in strong winds (i.e. tighter than just taking up the slack after the mainsheet is pulled block to block).

In certain conditions such as beating in heavy weather or sailing in a choppy sea the mast bend can be retained with the kicking strap while the mainsheet (and boom) is eased out to reduce the hook-back of the leech.

Going faster

Fast beating is essential for racing since the majority of races start on a beat. Here are some points to watch and ideas to try:

- Never allow the boat to heel excessively.

- Sit out hard in strong winds. Only ease

If you have the race control lines, this is how you tension the kicking strap (vang) and downhaul while beating.

When sailing in waves it is virtually impossible to stop water coming into the cockpit. If you get a chance, kick the water out of the back of the cockpit. It will be quicker than relying on the self bailer, but remember it is illegal in a race.

Good beating The daggerboard is right down, the down-haul is pulled to remove most (but not all) of the creases. The outhaul is off so that the gap between the sail and the boom is from your fingertips to half way up your wrist.

the mainsheet as a last resort.

- Keep the mainsheet pulled in tight except in light or very strong winds.

- Watch the front of the sail like a hawk. Keep trying to luff up, yet bear away every time the sail starts to flap.

- Keep a good look-out for other boats

- Watch for windshifts.

BEATING IN LIGHT WINDS
Patience and stealth are the order of the day. Move around the boat as little as possible; when you must, move slowly taking care not to shake the shape out of the sail.

Setting the horse and mainsheet
Ease the traveller a tiny amount in very light

winds (only). With the mainsheet now eased a little the boom will still stay approximately over the corner of the transom. Always remember that maximum speed through the water is more important than good pointing in these conditions since a well-sailed boat can quite easily go twice as fast as a badly-sailed one.

Steering
Continuously watch the luff of the sail, bearing away immediately if it begins to lift.

Trim
Sit over the well between the daggerboard and the leeward deck with your knees bent double and your legs along the leeward sidedeck (see photos below). This heels the boat which helps fill the sail (by gravity) and reduce hull-to-water skin friction. Heel the boat until the leeward gunwale

Good light wind technique.

is nearly under water. The lighter you are, the further to leeward you need to move.

Sail controls

The downhaul (Cunningham) should be loose.

The outhaul should be normal (i.e. 50 mm of draft in the middle of the foot) and tightened in extremely light winds to help keep what wind there is moving over the sail.

BEATING IN STRONG WINDS

Even with the easy-to-handle Topper this can be hard work, yet very rewarding. Sit out hard and aim for speed rather than close sailing to the wind – especially in waves which tend to stop the boat.

Setting the horse and mainsheet

The traveller must be pulled as tight as possible so that when the mainsail is sheeted in hard (bending the mast and flattening the sail) the boom will not come too close to the centreline of the boat and cause excessive heeling forces and drag. Ease the sail to spill wind only when the boat heels beyond 5°.

Steering over waves

Try to steer so that the boat has an easy passage over the waves, luffing as you go up the wave and bearing away as you dip back down.

Daggerboard

When it is difficult to hold the boat upright, or if it luffs of its own accord, you will find it helps to raise the board to the first or even the second notch. This reduces heeling by allowing the boat to slip sideways.

Trim

Sit out as hard as possible keeping reasonably far forward – waves permitting. This reduces weather helm by tilting the sail's centre of effort forward of the daggerboard. Be ready to move aft or pivot backwards at the waist quickly if the bow begins to bury itself.

Gusts

Watch for gusts approaching. Sit out and be prepared to spill wind from the sail.

Sail controls

Pull the downhaul very tight and the outhaul tight. The kicking strap (vang) should be tight enough to bend the boom and eased a little off wind.

SORTING OUT PROBLEMS WHEN BEATING IN STRONG WINDS

The main problem is the boat luffing up (turning into the wind). Try:

- Pulling up the centreboard to at least the first notch.
- Pulling on loads of downhaul (pull as hard as you can).
- To prevent the daggerboard floating up, put progrip on the inside of the blow mouldings.
- To stop the boat filling up with water allow it to heel as a wave goes over the foredeck.

- If you get into irons (pointing into the wind) pull up the daggerboard and sit at the back. Keep the rudder straight and the boat will pivot about the rudder. You may need to push out the boom a bit, too. (See photos A-F above.)

BEATING; COMMON MISTAKES

G. The foot of the sail is too loose and will prevent you sailing close to the wind.

H. Mainsheet too far out. Again, this will prevent you pointing close to the wind.

I. Sitting too far back. Sitting further forward will stop the stern (back) of the boat dragging through the water.

J. This boat is heeled too much. The skipper will have to pull too hard on the tiller to keep the boat from luffing up (turning in to the wind). Hike out!

K. "Pinching" (Sailing too close to the wind) It looks good to start with because you point closer to your goal, but the boat will slow far too much.

11 Tacking

What is tacking?

The boat in Figure 1 is beating with the sail on the starboard side (a). The boat turns into the wind (b) and keeps turning until it is beating with the sail on the port side (c). This turn is called a tack.

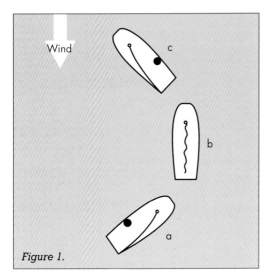

Figure 1.

Tacking in light to moderate winds

Never tack unless you are travelling at or near the maximum speed for the conditions.

Tacking with a centre mainsheet - shot from above.

If the boat has insufficient momentum you will come to a stop and blow backwards ('get into irons') before you can point the boat onto the new tack.

Tacking with the centre mainsheet - step by step

Both photo sequences on pages 48-49 show the manoeuvre with the centre mainsheet. Look for these steps:

1. Sail straight and pick up speed.
2. Push the tiller away firmly, lean back and begin to turn.
3. Stay on the old side and keep on turning.
4. Keep turning through the wind. The sail will begin to fill on the new side.
5. As the boat begins to heel in the new direction, cross the boat facing forwards and land on the "new" sidedeck. Straighten up (don't let the boat spin round too far onto a reach, you are trying to get to windward).
6. Use your weight to bring the boat flat, still steering with your hand behind your back.
7. Only when you are steering the boat properly on the new course should you change hands on the tiller extension and mainsheet. Do this by bringing the

Tacking with a centre mainsheet - shot from the foredeck.

mainsheet hand (still holding the mainsheet) to the tiller extension.

8. Transfer your old tiller hand around your body to the mainsheet.

9. Hike (sit out), and pull in the mainsheet. Take a bow!

Tacking with the stern mainsheet - step by step

(photo sequence pages 50-51)

1. Push the tiller gently but firmly away from you and at the same time sit out on the windward side.

2. Ease the mainsheet slightly and place it under the thumb of the hand that is holding the tiller extension. Let go with the other hand.

3. As the boat begins to roll on top of you, start to move to the opposite side. Face the stern of the boat as you move, pushing the tiller extension in front of your body. As you reach the halfway point take the tiller in your 'new' steering hand and grasp the mainsheet in your 'new' sheet hand.

4. As the boat turns through the eye

Tacking with a stern mainsheet, shot from behind ▲ and from above ▼.

of the wind and begins to heel in the new direction, 'land' on the other deck.

5 Sit on the new side, steer straight ahead and pull in the mainsheet once again. Check that you are on a good close-hauled course by observing the luff of the sail (and wind indicator).

Tacking in strong winds

It is very easy to stall the boat in heavy weather. Here are some precautions to help avoid this.

- Always tack when travelling at maximum speed.

- Raise the daggerboard to the first or second notch to reduce weather helm.

- Push the tiller over hard.

- As the sail comes over dive across the boat as quickly as possible, easing the mainsheet 150 mm.

- Sit out hard with your body weight well forward to counter the weather helm, and sheet in again.

TACKING
– SOME COMMON MISTAKES

A. Wait until the boat is head to wind before you cross to the 'new' side.

B. If you straighten up too soon the boat will stop, pointing into the wind. Keep turning, "through" the wind

C. But don't turn too far. Here the boat has swung round onto a reach after the tack, and may capsize.

D. With a centre mainsheet tack facing forwards!

12 Running

What is running?

Both boats in Figure 1 are running – i.e. they are sailing with the wind directly behind.

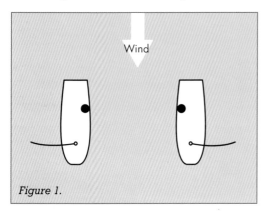

Figure 1.

Adjusting the sail

In medium and light winds the mainsheet should be out so that the boom is at 90^0 to the boat. In strong winds, when the boat tends to roll, pull the mainsheet in a little – but remember that the boat goes fastest with the sail right out. Don't forget to tie a knot in the end of the mainsheet!

Trim

Except in heavy winds or big waves sit forward in the cockpit and lean out to heel the boat to windward. In this way you will be able to steer a straight course with very little use of the rudder and also have the minimum wetted area.

Steering

It is vital to avoid an unexpected gybe (gybing is discussed in chapter 13). Watch the burgee carefully and avoid turning so that the wind is blowing from the same side

as the boom (Figure 2). This is 'running by the lee' – the wind is able to get behind the boom and flip it across. If you find yourself in this position, quickly push the tiller away from you for a moment; then straighten up.

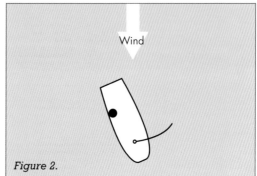

Figure 2.

Daggerboard

Pull the daggerboard almost right up when running, leaving only a few inches in the water. The exception is in heavy winds when half board will help to damp any rolling. Remember to lower the daggerboard sufficiently for it not to foul the kicking strap when gybing.

Gusts

As a gust arrives the boat will tend to roll so pull in the mainsheet and put down a little more daggerboard. Counter the boat's tendency to tip on top of you by luffing slightly. If the boat heels to leeward bear away a little.

Sail controls

The kicking strap (vang) should be 'normal' (page 18). Ease the downhaul to give plenty of curve in the sail.

Going faster

This is one point of sailing where it is an advantage to be behind another boat, since you can blanket the boat in front of you and catch it up.

Here are some points to watch and ideas to try:

- Let the mainsheet out so the boom is at right angles to the boat or even further out.

- Make sure you have the daggerboard well up.

- Heel the boat to windward until the 'pull' on the tiller stops.

- When a gust comes, run straight downwind with it. Try to stay with the gust as long as possible. If you see a gust to one side of the course, sail over to it and then ride it.

- Try to surf on waves as much as you can. Pull the mainsheet in a little as the boat accelerates down each wave (because the wind direction comes forward as you speed up).

For once you don't want to sail the boat flat!
If you do sail flat, the centre of effort of the
sail is to the side of the boat so makes it luff
up (turn into the wind).

Centre
of effort

Far better to heel the boat to windward,
bringing the centre of effort more directly
above the axis of the boat. This removes the
turning effect. You can even steer the boat
by altering the heel, keeping the rudder
straight. (If the boat heels towards you it
will turn away from you, and vice-versa.)

RUNNING IN LIGHT WINDS

*Sit forward and heel to windward. Hold the
daggerboard with your mainsheet hand to stop
you falling out.*

Trim
Sit well forward. Heel the boat to windward
holding the boom right out with your hand.

If the wind is so light that the sail falls out of
shape it may be better to heel the boat to
leeward, but watch the mainsheet doesn't
drag in the water! Alternatively, let the sail out
more than 90 degrees, hold it out with your
foot and heel to windward. The sail will "fall"
forward to windward and will hold its shape.

Steering
Use the tiller as little as possible.

Sail controls
All sail controls should be loose to give
a full sail.

RUNNING IN STRONG WINDS

Steering

Don't be in a hurry to get on a run when the wind is really blowing. Steer round gradually from a reach, letting the sail out slowly as you do so. Move back in the boat to help the bow lift.

If the boat starts to roll as you come onto the run, quickly pull the mainsheet back in a little. Keep a firm hand on the tiller, and don't let the boat turn back onto a reach.

Running by the lee is a little risky for the unwary and can result in an unexpected gybe, but it can be a very effective way to avoid nosediving into a wave. The technique is to luff a little to catch a wave as it comes up behind you, then bear off quickly down the face of it. If, as you shoot down, the bow looks as though it's going to bury itself in the wave ahead, sheet in and bear away further. The act of bearing off just before an imminent nosedive reduces the pressure in the sail (as does sheeting in) and greatly reduces the tendency for the bow to go under. But do watch the accidental gybe!

Adjusting the sail

Rolling is caused particularly by the top of the sail twisting forward in a gust and pushing the boat over to windward. If this

is likely to happen, pull on more kicking strap (vang) before the run starts.

If the boat does roll, pull in the mainsheet. In any case, beware of letting the mainsheet out too far on a hairy run. Keep the daggerboard at least half down to dampen rolling.

Sail controls

If it is really blowing it is not worth easing the sail controls except the downhaul (right off) – you won't gain much and time will be lost resetting on the next leg of the course.

Trim

Sit halfway between the daggerboard and the back of the cockpit.

RUNNING
– SOME COMMON MISTAKES ▼

Sit back in strong winds! Sheet in and bear away if the boat begins to nosedive. You should have put on more kicking strap (vang) for these conditions.

Spot the deliberate mistake! (Don't let the sail out too far.)

Kicking strap (vang) too loose. The sail is losing drive and may force the boat to heel to windward

13 Gybing

What is gybing?

In Figure 1, boat (a) is running with the sail on the starboard side. The helmsman turns through a small angle (b) and the wind forces the sail out to the port side of the boat (c). This turn is called a gybe.

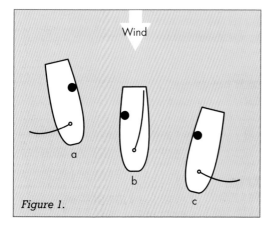

Wind

a

b

c

Figure 1.

Why is gybing difficult?

Gybing is the hardest sailing manoeuvre. Unlike tacking, the wind pushes on the sail throughout the turn. The boat is moving at high speed, so is very sensitive to tiller movements. A miscalculation results in the boat rolling – with the sail 'edge on' there's not much to dampen the roll and the helmsman tends to take an involuntary dip.

Decide when you want to gybe, and then do it! The best moment is when the boat is moving fast down a wave – since you're travelling away from the wind, the pressure on the sail is lessened.

Eight steps to a good gybe – centre mainsheet

1. **Get ready** Push the daggerboard half down (never gybe with the board right up or right down).
2. **Trim** Make sure the boat is flat or heeling slightly to windward.
3. **Turn** Turn slowly away from the wind until it is directly behind you. By now the boat will be heeling to windward.
4. **Mainsheet** Pump the mainsheet to start the boom moving.
5. **Duck** and cross the boat, facing forwards, as the boom comes across.
6. **Land** As you land on the new side, straighten the tiller. This stops the boat turning through too large an angle. You should find yourself sitting with the tiller

Get ready.   *Turn.*   *Keep the boat flat.*   *Look at the flag.*   *Pull the mainsh...*

How to change hands on the tiller extension and mainsheet

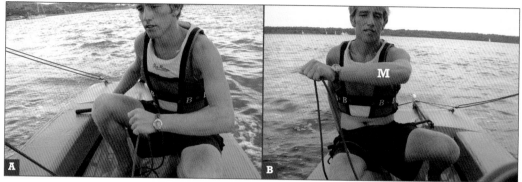

A. Ready to gybe.

B. Land on the new side. The tiller extension is behind your back.

C. Take the mainsheet hand (M) across your body and grab the tiller, still holding the mainsheet.

D. Let go with your old tiller hand (T) and grab the mainsheet.

behind your back and the mainsheet held across your body.

7. **Steer** Pull the tiller towards you to get back on course.

8. **Smile** You made it! If the boat rolls, pull in the mainsheet: otherwise let it out to the normal running position. Finally, when the boat is under control, change hands on the tiller and the mainsheet and bring the tiller extension across your body.

Cross the boat.

Land on the new deck.

Straighten up (tiller behind back).

Change hands.

Gybing – stern mainsheet

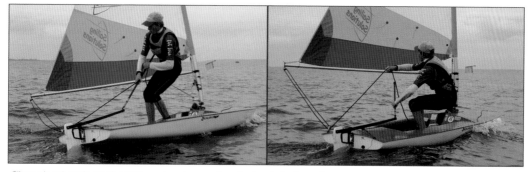

Changing hands on the tiller extension and mainsheet, facing aft.

Six steps to a good gybe – stern mainsheet

1. **Get ready.** Push the daggerboard half down (never gybe with the board right up or right down). Bear away until the wind is almost directly behind the boat.
2. **Pull in the mainsheet.** Pull in an arm's length of mainsheet, face aft, and heel the boat to windward (if you let it heel away from you, you can't turn).
3. **Change hands.** Clamp the mainsheet under the thumb of the hand holding the tiller extension. Let go with the other hand.
4. **Turn.** Bear away further until the boom comes across (don't forget to duck!) At the same time grip the leeward gunwale with your free hand.
5. **Cross the boat.** As the boom comes over, cross the boat facing aft. Reach under the mainsheet and grasp the tiller extension with your free hand. Lift the mainsheet with your other hand, giving a short pull to prevent the sheet fouling up on the rudder stock.
6. **Straighten up.** 'Reverse' the tiller hard to bring the boat back on course.

Gybing in strong winds
When the wind is very strong it is safer (though slower) to gybe without pulling in any mainsheet before the gybe. You will need to bear away a lot further before the sail comes over but when it does it will just fly harmlessly out on the other side like a

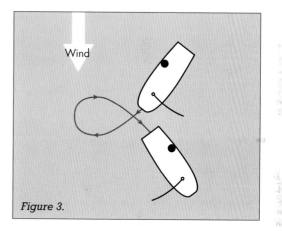

Wind

Figure 3.

flag. As you bear away again onto the new run be careful that the boat doesn't roll on top of you!

If you consider that a capsize is almost inevitable you may prefer to wear round. This involves turning through almost 360° as shown in Figure 3. Do this with the daggerboard half up; pull in the mainsheet and spin the boat around fast.

GYBING – SOME COMMON MISTAKES

It is useless to go into a gybe heeling to leeward. The heeled boat tries to turn the wrong way. Before these skippers can gybe they will need to let out some mainsheet, bear away and heel the boat towards them as they turn.

If you gybed like this in a breeze, you could get rather damp! You should centralise the tiller as the boom comes over and keep your weight low and aft. Be prepared to prevent the boat luffing up (slewing around into the wind).

14 Taking a penalty

A

The two turns penalty

If you have a collision with someone in a race and are in the wrong you have to do two circles, known in the trade as the Two Turns Penalty. You have to include two tacks and two gybes.

If you hit a buoy, you have to do one turn, including a tack and a gybe.

You are going to do plenty of these as you learn to race, so now that you can tack and gybe why not practise sailing in circles? The photo sequence shows a one turn penalty.

B

C

D

E

15 Capsizing

Everyone capsizes. Indeed, if you don't capsize sometimes, you're probably not really trying!

When the inevitable happens, try to stay on top of the boat. In most other classes, the crew needs to swim to right the boat!

In the Topper this is unnecessary.

Even if the boat turns upside-down, this is no problem in a Topper (see photo sequence on pages 64-5). Climb on the hull, stand with your back to the wind and lever the boat onto its side. Try to stay on the

Recovering from a capsize to leeward

daggerboard; you can then right the boat as described below.

If you do fall off the daggerboard, try pulling down on it while you are in the water. If this fails, swim round and use the mast as a step to get yourself on top of the boat. Then begin again!

Never leave the boat (to swim for the shore, for example). The hull will support you almost indefinitely – it has reserve buoyancy inside and will float even if the skin is punctured and it is more easily spotted than a swimmer. The boat will tip one of two ways: to leeward (which is more pleasant) or to windward.

Capsizing to leeward
As the boat capsizes climb over the side and

onto the daggerboard, then lean back and slowly pull the boat upright. The boat automatically turns into the wind. At the last moment, straddle the deck and scramble into the cockpit.

Avoiding a capsize to leeward

● Watch for gusts.

● Keep the mainsheet in your hand at all times.

● Sit out hard in strong winds.

● On a reach or run, avoid letting the boat turn into the wind.

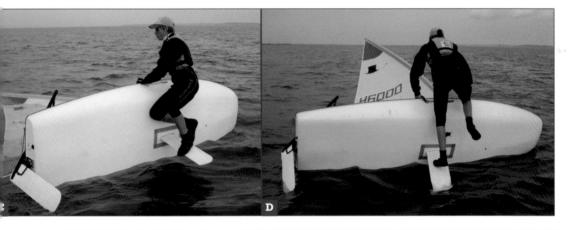

Recovering from a capsize to windward

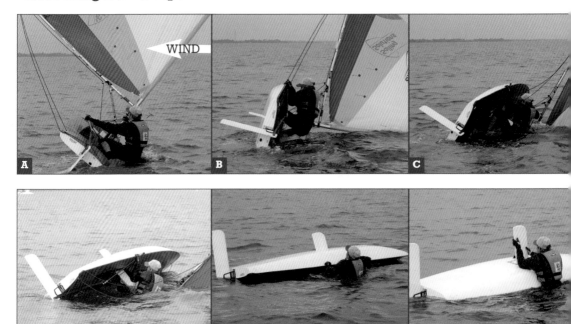

Capsizing to windward

Try to stay on top of the boat. However, you may well fall out as the boat capsizes to windward. If this happens on a reach or run, hang on to the mainsheet at all costs – the boat is travelling fast and might finish up some distance away. The mainsheet is your lifeline. Do not hang on to the tiller extension which might snap as you go over the side.

Pull yourself back to the boat along the mainsheet. In these circumstances the

Topper will almost certainly have inverted.

1. Climb onto the upturned boat with your back to the wind.
2. Pull the daggerboard right out.
3. Stand on the gunwale (lip) with your back to the wind.
4. With your hands around the board, lever the boat upright until you can scramble onto the daggerboard.
5. Right the boat!

In shallow water, don't let the boat turn upside down or the mast may snap.

If the mast gets stuck in mud, stand on the daggerboard close to the hull and gently bounce up and down to free it.

Avoiding a capsize to windward

- Be ready to move your weight inboard in lulls.

- Pull in the mainsheet rapidly if the boat rolls to windward.

- On a reach or run, avoid turning fast away from the wind.

Getting going again

After righting, the boat will normally be head-to-wind. To get moving, lift the daggerboard, push out the boom and wait for the boat to swing away from the wind.

Then push the down the daggerboard, sheet in and away we go! (See page 47.)

Recovering from turning turtle (photos J - O)

16 Landing

Think ahead before landing since a great deal of damage can result if you don't take care. Always try to land on a windward shore (wind blowing from shore to sea) if you can because this makes it easier to stop!

Landing on a windward shore

1. Sail slowly towards the shore. Control the boat's speed by letting out the mainsheet. Ease the horse (traveller) so the tiller can be raised to pull up the rudder later.
2. At the last minute, turn into the wind and quickly lift out the daggerboard and raise the rudder as you stop (figure 1).
3. Step into the water on the shore side of the boat, holding it as near the bow as you can.

Landing on a lee shore

There may be times when landing on a lee shore is unavoidable. In this case approach the shore on the reach which is closest to the wind direction (figure 2). Raise the daggerboard and rudder as far as possible while still keeping control. Let the sail out so that it is

Landing on a lee shore.

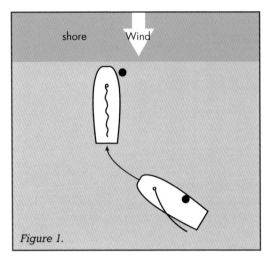

Figure 1.

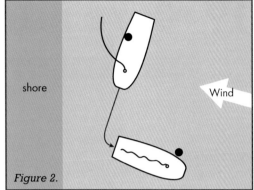

Figure 2.

half flapping and not causing the boat to heel or go particularly fast. Sail in as close to the shore as the depth of water will allow before luffing head to wind, jumping out and holding the boat by the bow. Ask someone on the shore to bring you your launching trolley.

In surf, this method doesn't work! (The boat will probably swing broadside to the waves and get rolled up the beach.) The technique here is to pull up the rudder and daggerboard and sail fast through the surf, straight towards the beach. Keep going straight until the bow grounds, jump out and then drag the boat up the beach before the next wave arrives.

17 Care and maintenance

STORAGE

With a hull depth of only 380 mm, the Topper is very easy to store and takes up a very small space. If you are storing out of doors it is perfectly satisfactory to stand the boat on its gunwale against a wall; you can pull it against the wall by passing a rope out through the daggerboard case and tightening this on to a piece of timber set at right angles to the slot. If you have room to keep the boat flat, raise it off the ground a few inches to allow air to circulate. (The photographs show the best support points.) There is no need to cover the boat – foul weather will have no detrimental effect at all on the polypropylene hull.

If you have the use of a garage, there is usually enough height to sling a Topper from the roof above the car. You can use the roof rack straps as slings and these should pass around the hull – forward beneath the mast step position and aft below the rear bulkhead. The easiest method of lifting the boat into the required position is to drive it into the garage on the car roof. This way you have the minimum of lifting to contend with!

ROUTINE MAINTENANCE

Hull

The material from which Topper hulls are moulded is extremely tough and is the same all the way through. So you are not concerned – as with a GRP hull – about damaging the gelcoat and allowing water to penetrate. However, polypropylene is a little softer than GRP and is inclined to scratch with harsh treatment. With sensible use and reasonable care, it is quite feasible to keep the bottom in good shape; minor scuffs and scratches can be removed with fine wet-and-dry paper, and a reasonable shine can be restored with a good cutting compound. More severe scratches are best tackled with a sharp cabinet scraper or even a very sharp, very finely set smoothing plane. The material cuts beautifully but does not respond well to coarse sanding, which can leave a furry surface which will do nothing for your boatspeed. Major shunts – usually the result of a boat becoming detached from its roof rack – can result in a split hull. This can be satisfactorily repaired by a special hot-air welding process and the manufacturers will advise on your nearest specialist.

Spars

These should rarely require any maintenance although it is a good idea to check the riveted eyes for security – particularly if you are going out in heavy weather. Rivets have been known to break or work loose. Cleats can also break or 'burn out', but make sure you check the class rules thoroughly to ensure that you do not replace them with anything that could put you out of class.

Rudder and daggerboard

These are injection moulded in polypropylene, and glass-reinforced to give them the required stiffness and hard

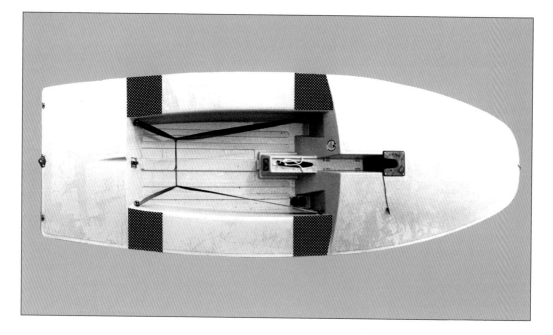

surface. No maintenance at all is required apart from keeping the tips smooth and free of indentations by the judicious use of wet-and-dry paper. Always check the rudder bolts for correct tightness – there should be no slop between the blade and the cast aluminium stock, nor should it be so tight so as to prevent the blade from retracting properly. Tiller extensions have been known to detach themselves at the least convenient moments so it is worth checking frequently that the connecting bolt is secure and properly locked.

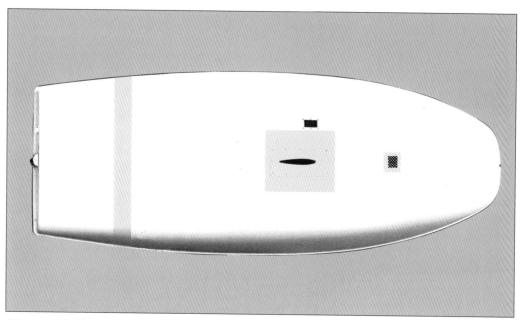

Strong points. The aft one is under the aft bulkhead.

Sail

This is the 'engine' of your Topper and if you race the boat it is absolutely essential to keep it in peak 'tune'. There is no doubt that all sails have a life-span, so according to how often you use your Topper you will have to replace the sail from time to time. Nevertheless, sensible treatment and care can extend this life-span considerably. Never crumple a sail into its bag after use – always fold it carefully, concertina fashion across the sail parallel to the boom, finally rolling it up as loosely as possible. An even better system is to roll the sail around a plastic pipe, which is slightly less convenient to transport but does totally eliminate creasing. Creasing will not ruin the sail, but could make it that little bit less efficient.

Salt water will have no short-term ill-effects but always rinse the sail thoroughly in fresh water and dry properly prior to storage.

Fastenings

There are a number of machine screws on the Topper's hull and these are threaded into expanding brass inserts which work in a similar fashion to a rawlplug. They should be checked periodically for tightness but be careful not to overtighten.

Self bailer and mast gate

These do not need lubrication but it helps to keep them operating efficiently if you rinse them frequently with fresh water to clear away any abrasive sand and grit that could shorten their lives, and spray with a 'dry' ptfe spray..

Tips on travel and storage

Topper hulls distort when left for long periods of time. Try to store them upside-down. The decks seem to distort less than the hulls and anyway don't matter so much in a racing boat.

Choose a trolley that supports the hull under the back of the daggerboard case and under the mast step. It should also have a high handle to save your back and allow the boat to be stored on its deck. The original plastic trolley is very poor. Galvanised steel and lightweight aluminium ones are far better. The latter are "knockdown" which is great if you plan to car-top. A good top cover will also fit as a bottom cover but increasingly sailors are using undercovers as well. These should allow water to escape either by having mesh panels or be made of a material that allows water to seep through. Undercovers protect from the worst of road dirt but more importantly save abrasion.

Foil covers and spar bags are readily available and do make life easier.

Trollies are available that fit the normal Laser combi base and this is a good move if you plan to move on to a Laser. There are lots of double and triple stacker trailers around. It is great if a box is included in the design.

18 The International Topper Class Association

The Topper is one of the world's fastest-growing dinghy classes and enjoys one of the best-supported and best-administered class associations.

The International Topper Class Association (ITCA) has divisions in many countries. Membership is mandatory to be eligible for ITCA events.

There are many benefits of belonging to ITCA: members receive free of charge the quarterly magazine *Topper Times* which gives full information and reports on Topper events, regattas and other social activities. The association defines (and polices) the rules of the class – making sure that racing is fair and that the older boats remain competitive. And, perhaps most important of all, the association will help you communicate with other Topper sailors and thus enjoy your boat to the full – whether you are a beginner or a budding world champion!

The addresses of your National and International Secretaries can be obtained from the manufacturers:

Topper International Limited
Kingsnorth Technology Park
Wotton Road
Ashford
Kent
TN23 6LN
England

www.toppersailboats.com

Also www.gbrtopper.co.uk

Part 2
The small rig

Part 2
The small rig

The 4.2 sail is nearly 20% smaller than the standard one. The area has been taken out of the leech (back of the sail) making the boat better balanced in a breeze. The end of the boom is three inches higher, so there is less tendency for the boom to hit the water when the boat heels on a reach. And if you do capsize, the boat is far easier to right because there is less sail area to drag through the water.

This rig is designed for younger sailors who find the Topper a handful. But all the feedback is that it is a great rig for everyone, and older skippers find it a delight in a blow. Indeed, in a regatta or series you can choose to use the 4.2 rig and sail against the standard boats provided you stick to your chosen rig throughout – the 'single sail rule'. It might be worth considering this at a windy venue! As the sail becomes more popular there will eventually be a 4.2 division at regattas, with a 4.2 champion and separate trophies.

Apart from the sail, the rest of the gear is standard. And the settings are the same, too. (But, because the sail is cut flatter, you may not need to put such huge amounts of tension on the control lines.)

Part 3
Racing: the basics

Part 3
Racing: the basics

Don't forget that, beginner or not, you will be a very welcome addition to the fleet. Those who usually do well, the 'hotshots', will be only too pleased to come home having beaten a larger fleet. Those nearer the back will welcome the chance to perhaps beat someone! Don't be disappointed if you finish last – just give it a go. Do remember that, particularly in the heat of the start, some competitors can get a bit excited and may shout at you if they think you are infringing the rules. Don't let this worry you; they may not have had time to realise that you are a beginner and you will probably find that back in the clubhouse they are quite friendly. But do speak to them about any such incident afterwards, particularly if you are unsure of which rule you may have infringed. It's a good chance to learn as well as make friends.

THE RULES

A full discussion of the rules is outside the scope of this book: see *The Rules in Practice* by Bryan Willis. For the cautious beginner, a few key rules will keep you out of trouble in most cases.

Boats meeting on opposite tacks

A boat is either on a port tack or a starboard tack. It is on a port tack if the wind is blowing over its port side. In figure 1, boats A, B and C are on port tack; boats D, E and F are on starboard tack.

A port tack boat must keep clear of a starboard tack boat.

D, E and F have right of way over A, B and C, who must keep clear.

Boats meeting on the same tack

If the boats are overlapped (i.e. if the bow of the following boat is ahead of a line at right angles to the stern of the leading boat) the following rule applies:

A windward boat shall keep clear of a leeward boat.

In Figure 2, G must keep clear of H, I must keep clear of J and L must keep clear of K.

If the boats are not overlapped (figure 3):

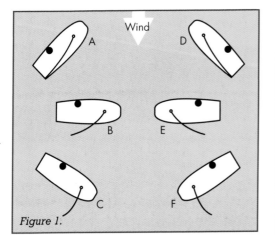

Figure 1.

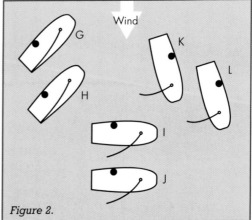

Figure 2.

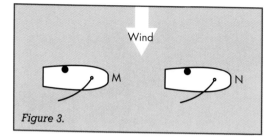

Figure 3.

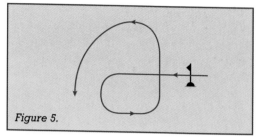

Figure 5.

A boat clear astern shall keep clear of a boat clear ahead.

If M is sailing faster it is not allowed to sail into the back of N.

Boats meeting at marks

An outside boat shall give each boat overlapping it on the inside room to round or pass the mark.

P must give O room to go round the mark on the inside. O must get his overlap on P before P's bow reaches an imaginary circle of radius two boat's lengths from the mark (figure 4).

Note that this rule does not apply at starts (see page 78).

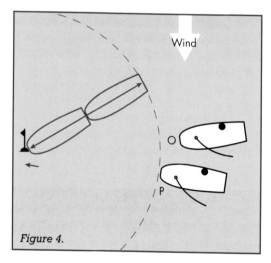

Figure 4.

Penalties

If you hit a mark, you must sail clear and do a one turn penalty including a tack and a gybe (figure 5) (see chapter 14) . You have no rights while you are doing this penalty turn.

If you hit another boat and reckon you're

in the right, shout 'protest'. Argue your case in the protest room afterwards.

If you hit another boat and are in the wrong, you may exonerate yourself by sailing clear and doing a two turn penalty. (see chapter 14). You have to do two tacks and two gybes (figure 6).

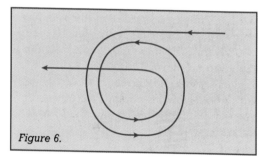

Figure 6.

THE LINE START

The start is the most important part of the race. If you get a bad start, you have to overtake everyone to win – while you're battling past the opposition, the leaders are sailing further ahead. If you get a good start, you're sailing in clear air.

How is a race started?

Most races are started on a beat. The race committee sets an (imaginary) start line, usually between the mast of the committee boat (A) and a buoy (B) (figure 7). They often lay another buoy (C), which does not have to be on the line. Boats are not allowed to sail between C and A.

Normally five minutes before the start the class flag is raised on the committee boat and a gun is fired. Four minutes before the start the blue peter is raised and a sound signal is made.

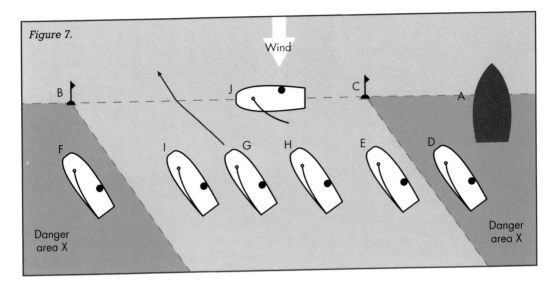

Figure 7.

One minute before the start the Blue Peter is lowered and a long sound signal is made.

At the start, the class flag is lowered and a sound signal is made.

Boats must be behind the start line when the starting signal is made. Your aim is to be just behind the line, sailing at full speed, at the start.

How can I get a good start?

Set your watch at the five-minute signal, and check it at the four-minute signal.

During the last few minutes, avoid the 'danger' areas X and Y. From X you cannot get on to the start line because the boats to leeward have right of way. Boat D, for example, will be forced the wrong side of buoy C. In Y you are bound to pass the wrong side of buoy B. Boat F has this problem.

Don't go too far from the line – 30 yards is plenty. A wall of boats builds up on the line in the last two minutes, and you must be in that wall. If you're behind it, not only can you not get in, but your wind is cut off by the wall.

Aim to be six boat lengths behind the line with 45 seconds to go – closer if boats to windward are moving ahead of you. Control your speed with careful use of the mainsheet. Keep the boat moving forward

slowly – most of the sail will be flapping but take care not to stop or you will have no steerage way. With ten seconds to go you should be two lengths behind the line. Pull in the mainsheet, sit out and start beating. You should cross the line just after the gun with full speed. Boat G has followed this advice.

What about the other boats?

It's important to watch out for other boats as you line up to start. G has right of way over H, but must keep clear of I. As you line up, keep turning into the wind a little. This keeps you away from the boat to leeward – it also opens up a nice 'hole' to leeward that you can sail down into at the start (for extra speed).

Don't reach down the line with 15 seconds to go like boat J. You will have no rights over G, H and I who will sail into you. If you're too early, let the sail out in good time and slow down.

Which end of the line should I start?

So far, the wind has been at right angles to the start line. As far as the wind is concerned it will not matter where on the line you start.

Usually, however, the wind is not at right angles to the line. You can find out what it's doing by sailing down the line on a reach. Adjust the sail so the front just flaps (Figure 8).

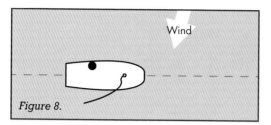

Figure 8.

Keeping the mainsheet in the same position, tack and reach back down the line.

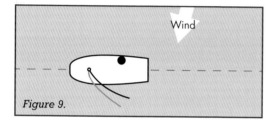

Figure 9.

In Figure 9, the sail will now be too far in – you will have to let the mainsheet out to make it flap. This indicates the wind is blowing from the starboard end of the line – and you should start at this end.

How do I make a starboard end start?

Sail slowly, and as close to the wind as possible, so you will reach the windward end of the line with the gun (figure 10). Boats to windward have no rights and are

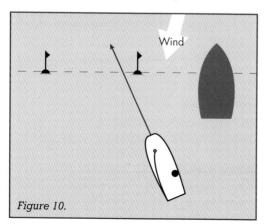

Figure 10.

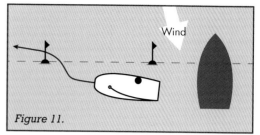

Figure 11.

forced out. Boats to leeward can't touch you – you're already sailing as close to the wind as possible.

How do I make a port end start?

Keep near the port end of the line (figure 11). Aim to cross as near the buoy as possible. Tack onto port tack as soon as you can clear the fleet.

THE GATE START

A gate start is made by crossing the wake of a boat called the pathfinder which is beating on port tack in front of the fleet. In theory everyone has an equally good start, because the earlier you start the further you have to sail.

The pathfinder, who is selected by the race committee from among the competitors, waits near the committee boat while the usual sound and flag signals are made. About one minute before the start the pathfinder sets off on port tack, accompanied by two motor boats, the gate boat and guard boat, to protect it from overenthusiastic competitors (see figure 12). A few seconds before the

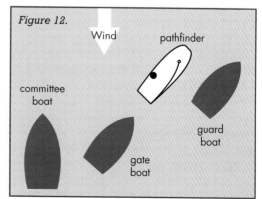

Figure 12.

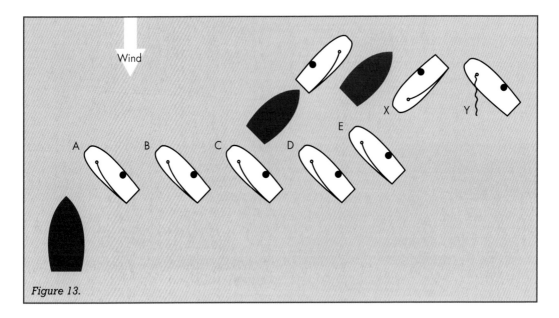

Figure 13.

start a free-floating buoy is dropped over the back of the gate boat to mark the port (left-hand) end of the line. After the start, competitors (on starboard tack) pass closely behind the gate boat (figure 13). The line gradually lengthens, and boats start one at a time. A late start is no disadvantage, since the pathfinder is sailing up the beat for you while you're waiting.

How can I get a good start?

You need to know the course the pathfinder will take. So, with about four minutes to go, begin beating on port tack from the committee boat. After two or three minutes bear away onto a reach, then tack and wait with your sail flapping (like boat Y in figure 13). Watch for the pathfinder, and control your speed so that you beat slowly up to the stern of the guard boat. As you go behind it, pick up speed by bearing away slightly and sitting out. Then beat, flat out, to pass just behind the stern of the gate boat.

NEVER reach towards the guard boat like boat X. You have no rights over boats D and E who will push you into the guard boat or gate boat. If you hit either, you will be disqualified. If you find yourself in boat X's

position, try to tack onto port and bear away. When you're ready, tack back onto starboard and try again. If all else fails, point into the wind and stop!

How can I recover from a bad start?

If you start too far from the gate boat, your only option is to sail through the gate, then tack onto port and sail behind the whole fleet to the right-hand side of the course. If that turns out to be the best side, you could find yourself ahead at the windward mark!

Where should I start?

Start late if you think you are slower than the pathfinder, if you think the pathfinder will hit a permanent header (see page 82) or if the tide is more favourable to the right of the course. Otherwise start early.

THE BEAT

After the tension of the start, it's important to settle down and concentrate on sailing hard.

What about other boats?

A boat when beating casts a 'wind shadow' – shown in figure 14. It also creates an area of disturbed air to windward due to the

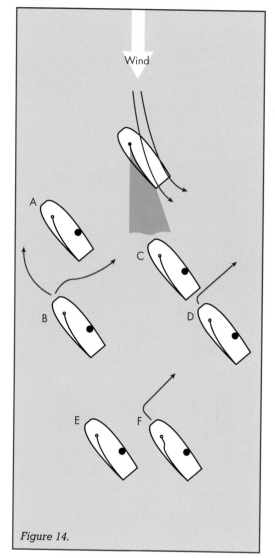

Figure 14.

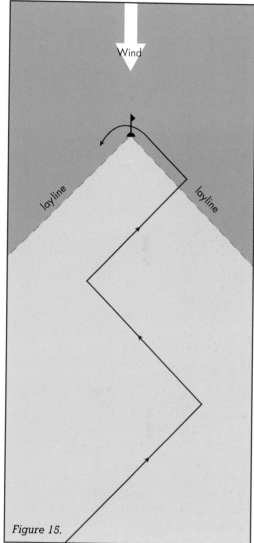

Figure 15.

wind being deflected by the sail; the air behind the boat is also disturbed.

You should therefore avoid sailing just to windward of another boat, behind it, or in its wind shadow. In diagram 14, boat B should either tack or bear away to clear its wind. Boats D and F should both tack.

Which way should I go?

You may have to modify your course to take account of tides and windshifts, but your first aim should be to make reasonably long tacks to start with, shortening them as you

approach the windward mark.

Don't sail into the area indicated by the shaded part of figure 15 – if you do, you will have to reach in to the buoy and will lose valuable time and distance. Stay inside the laylines – these are the paths you would sail when beating to hit the windward mark.

When approaching the windward mark on the first beat in a big fleet it is advisable not to arrive at the mark on port tack. For safety's sake make your final approach on starboard tack.

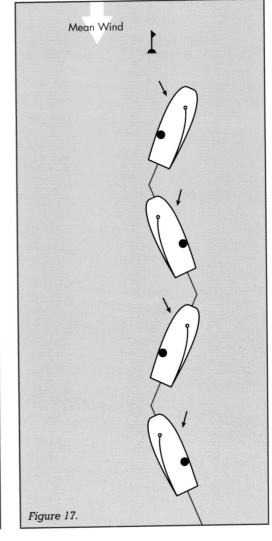

Figure 16.

Figure 17.

Windshifts

Once you are confident at beating and can tack efficiently, you are ready to start using windshifts.

The wind constantly alters in direction about its mean. Some of the shifts are more pronounced and last longer than others – it is these that you have to spot and use.

In shifty winds, stay close to the middle of the beat. Tack each time the wind heads you (forces you to alter course away from the mark). In Figure 16, the boat takes no account of windshifts. Note how little progress it makes compared with the boat

in Figure 17, which tacks each time the wind heads it.

The main problem is to differentiate between a real shift and a short-lived change in the wind. For that reason, sail on into each shift for five or ten seconds to make sure it's going to last. If a header lasts that long, tack.

If you find yourself tacking too often, or are confused, sail on one tack for a while until you're sure what the wind is doing. Remember that you lose at least a boat's length each time you tack, so there has to be a good reason to do so.

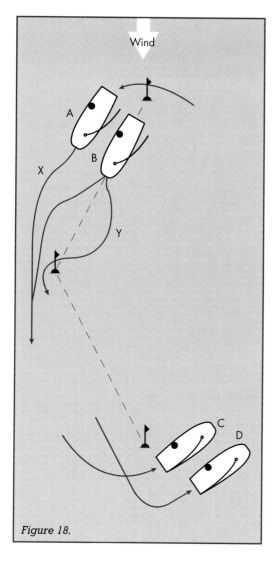

Figure 18.

What course should I steer?

The quickest way down the reach is a straight line from one mark to the next. However, if your rivals let you sail this course, you're lucky! The problem is that overtaking boats (e.g. A in figure 18) push up to windward. The boats to leeward (e.g. B) get nervous about their wind being stolen and steer high also. The result is that everyone sails an enormous arc (X), losing ground on the leaders.

You have to decide whether or not to go on the 'great circle'; the alternative is to sail a leeward path (Y). You have to go down far enough to avoid the blanketing effect of the boats to windward – but usually you will sail a shorter distance than they do. You can go for the leeward route on the second reach too, but this time you will be on the outside at the turn.

How can I get down the reach faster?

* Follow the tips for fast reaching on page 37, 'Going faster'.
* Keep your wind clear.
* Sail the shortest route.
* Go for the inside turn at marks.

Starting the next beat

As you approach the leeward mark, tighten the downhaul and push down the daggerboard. Steer round the mark so that you leave it very close (like boat C). Don't come in to the mark close (like boat D) or you'll start the beat well to leeward of your rivals. Sit out and go!

THE RUN

In strong winds, take your time as you bear away on to a run. Pull the daggerboard half up, sit back and adjust the mainsheet as you turn. If the boat starts to roll, steer a straight course and pull in the mainsheet a little. Continue to bear away when the boat is under control.

How can I get up the beat faster?

* Keep your wind clear.
* Watch for windshifts.
* Keep near the middle of the course.
* Practise tacking.
* Get fit – then you can sit out harder!

THE REACH

If it's blowing hard, pull the daggerboard half up before you bear away round the windward mark. Turn slowly, moving your weight back and letting out the mainsheet.

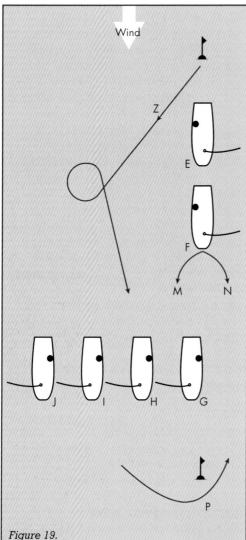

Figure 19.

What course should I steer?

The quickest route is a straight line to the leeward mark (figure 19).

In very strong winds, you may not be able to control the boat on a straight downwind run. An alternative is to follow course Z, wearing round (see page 59) rather than gybing at the midpoint.

The presence of other boats may also prevent your steering a straight course. Boat F is blanketed by boat E – it can escape by steering to one side (course M or N). Other things being equal, N would be better since it gives the inside turn at the next mark.

Boat E is correct to blanket F in this way. E can attack from a range of up to four boat's lengths; it can sail right up behind F, turning to one side at the last moment to overtake. E must, of course, keep clear of F during this manoeuvre.

Watch out for boats still beating, especially when running on port tack. Alter course in good time to avoid them – a last minute turn could capsize you.

What about crowding at the leeward mark?

It often happens that several boats arrive at the leeward mark together. The inside berth is the place to aim for – H, I and J have to give

Below: Practising starting. 'Hang' near a buoy with the sail flapping, using the tiller to control your position. Then sheet in and start on the signal.

G room to turn inside them. If you're in J's position, it's better to slow down and wait to turn close to the buoy rather than sail round the outside of the pack. Try to anticipate this situation, and slow down and move across to the inside in good time. Try to get G's position.

As you get near the leeward mark, tighten the downhaul and push the daggerboard down. Turn slowly and aim to leave the mark close (course P). You will need to pull in a good length of mainsheet as you round the mark – pull it in using both hands as described on page 35 and page 86.

How can I get down the run faster?

- Follow the 'Going faster' tips on page 53.
- Keep your wind clear.
- Sail the shortest route.
- Go for the inside turn at the leeward mark.

CURRENTS AND TIDES

When sailing, you must take account of currents and tides. Naturally, when sailing against the current you will look for a course where the current is weakest, and when you are sailing with the current you will go where it is strongest. The current is weakest in shallow water and near the shore (where friction with the land slows it down).

Before you go afloat make sure you know the likely strength and direction of the tides across the race course.

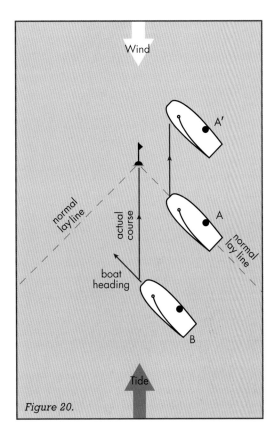

Figure 20.

Beating against the tide

Enormous gains can be made at the start over the majority of the competition who will disregard the effect of the tide. Get to the line early and stem the tide with the sail flapping – it is often possible to have a whole boat's length lead over boats around you in these circumstances.

Rounding the leeward mark.

Beating with the tide

Starting is difficult since in these circumstances the majority of the fleet will be early, resulting in many general recalls. You have no alternative but to keep in line with the front rank of starters.

Great gains can be made however on the beat and reach in wind-with-tide conditions. Figure 20 shows how easy it is to overstand the windward mark if you go to the normal layline; boat A expected just to lay the mark but is swept well upwind; boat B gets it right. You can gain many places by keeping near the middle of the course, always tacking well within the laylines.

On the reach, helms unaware of the effect of the tide will sail a considerably greater distance (figure 21). They may end up running into the tide like boat C – this is very slow! Boat D allows for the tidal effect and sails straight to the mark, even though her heading is well to leeward.

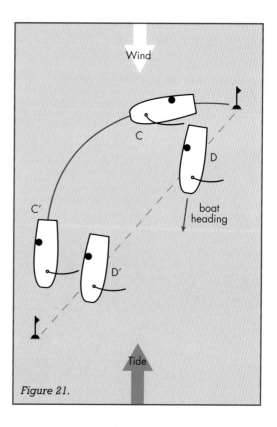

Figure 21.

Part 4
Masterclasses

Masterclass 1
Preparing yourself
for success

I will often ask a group I am coaching "Who would like to win boat races?" and they will all raise a hand. The next question is "Who *really* wants to win boat races?" and most will say they do. The number of hands goes down when you ask, "Who is *desperate* to win boat races?" and of course that is understandable. Sailing can be enjoyed in so many different ways and the way someone enjoys it can change over the years.

These masterclasses will give you the best chance of winning by preparing your boat and understanding how it works to achieve your best speed, preparing yourself physically and mentally, by giving you pointers to good race tactics and race strategy and by touching on goal setting. They also seek to provide a little advice to parents on how to support their youngsters as they develop as racers.

Sailing is not rocket science. The superstar who wins a boat race is not superhuman. Every part of sailing can be learned, none is difficult, it's just that there are very many parts to learn and then be applied at the right time!

The aim is to prioritise the things you learn so most progress can be made in the shortest time.

To win a particular boat race you must:
- Turn up!
- Have a reliable boat (but a technically well-prepared boat is helpful)

- Understand the Sailing Instructions
- Know the course

The most important techniques are:
- Starting – the most important 10 seconds in any race
- Upwind sailing – maintain clear air and look for the laylines
- Offwind sailing – clear air again but establish the transit
- Mark rounding – normally wide in tight out.

The most important boat handling/boatspeed techniques are:
- To think of the rudder as a brake – it stops you
- Use the shape of the boat and your sail to steer the boat
- Change your controls often and feel the results
- Practise, practise, practise and practise so that doing things well becomes automatic. Only then can you look outside the boat and take in the bigger tactical and strategic picture. This is where the biggest gains are to be made.

Attitude
There is no doubt that the most important 150 mm in any boat race is the space between the sailors right and left ears! You determine how successful you are going to be and it's not down to talent!

It is said the three factors that determine

success are talent, determination and funding but of the three I'd place determination the most important by far. Yes you need funding but if you are determined enough (and pleasant with it!) someone out there will help you, especially if you show you are prepared to help yourself as well.

Talent is useful but I'd back the determined sailor with less talent than a talented sailor with less determination. Clearly the top of the sport has talented sailors but they are talented sailors who also have determination – a wonderful combination!

So do you like to win, do you really want to win or are do you 'just have' to win? This will decide how much time and effort you will put in. The trick is to make the best use of the time you are prepared to spend.

Mental toughness

Mental toughness is all about being able to perform under pressure, in the race. Lots of sailors lack confidence in their ability and this stops them getting the results they deserve. Confidence is not about brashness, which too often shows

itself for the veneer that it is when things get difficult. Confidence develops over a period of time, based on adding to your abilities in all the many aspects of the great sport of sailing. I like the idea of a confidence bag, a place where all my process skills are collected. Knowing that I have these skills gives me the inner confidence to trust my ability and the knowledge that if I'm having a bad day that's all it is – a bad day – which is not the same as being a bad sailor. Results follow and these reinforce my confidence – a virtuous circle!

In the zone

When things are going well it's often referred to as being 'in the zone'. You feel good, the boat is fast, you're not concerned about the way others are going and the wind strength is just perfect for you. Being in 'the zone' is great, getting back there when things are not so good is the aim. Start by recognising how you react under pressure. Do you get 'hyper' and throw all your toys out of the cot (often associated with feeling tense and irritable and making rash decisions)? Do you close down and feel lethargic (often associated with not making any decisions and not being forceful enough)? Somewhere in between is where your best performance can be found. Hyper types need to calm down; lethargic types need to be stimulated.

I'm definitely the hyper type and amongst other things grip the tiller extension so hard I can't read what it's trying to tell me. I find the phrase 'soft hands' helps me remember what it's like in the zone and I find myself back there. Others tell me they sing when things are going well and they have particular songs for getting back in the zone for different conditions. Great idea – but you haven't heard my singing!

Things do go wrong in boat races and it's common to dwell on what's happened. In different situations you can find yourself thinking 'what if?'. What if I finish the race in this position? What if I capsize at this gybe mark? What if I lose the protest? None of these thoughts is useful. The aim is to concentrate on the next 100 m, on the next decision, on the next boat-handling task. Don't dwell on the past or even anything beyond the end of the race; aim to make everything you do the best it can be and the results will follow.

Goal setting

Fail to plan and you plan to fail.

Goal setting is a way of maximising the time you spend trying to improve as a sailor. All elite athletes set goals.

Long-term, inspirational, goal

These are your dreams, the things you want to achieve in any field of human activity. They may well change as you go along but without them you are going nowhere.

Medium term goals

These are associated with the coming season, the events you want to attend and the results you would like to achieve, and the squad you hope to be invited into. They will help you sort out the logistics for the year.

Short term goals

These are process goals – e.g. aiming to improve leeward mark roundings.

Goal setting makes the difference and so few sailors do it effectively. I love this quote from Ed Moses:

"Ain't no use worryin' bout things beyond your control, cause if they're beyond your control, ain't no use worryin' ...."

"Ain't no use worryin' bout things within your control, cause if you got them under control, ain't no use worryin' ...."

Knowing what you can control and what you can't is the key here. You can't control the weather and I hear sailors complaining that it's not their conditions and that they hate it. Like everyone I prefer 12 knots and sunny with a nice swell running but the trouble is everyone else loves it as well, can sail well in it and it's more difficult for me to win. No-one prefers 3 knots and rain with a nasty tide because it's difficult. If you remind yourself that others are hating it and can persuade yourself that you love it (or at least hate it less than them!) then psychologically you've got them beat. You get in the zone more quickly and you concentrate longer. The result is you find yourself doing well in these conditions and, as if by magic, you find that you do like these conditions. Equally, when it's really windy, don't think, 'I'm too light for these conditions'. Remember that everyone's hurting; keep going a little longer and again good results will come.

Your short term goals will be process based – improving tacking in light winds say or even better improving the entry phase of a roll tack or even better positioning your feet during the entry phase of a roll tack. Get it? – it's better to be specific.

There are loads of ways of setting this out in sailing.

But which process to improve on to get the most benefit?

Use this chart to help decide.

Aspect of Sailing	Position in the fleet of 10	Importance of that aspect /10	Result in the fleet of 100	How this result can be improved

Aspects of Sailing – list all the parts of all the elements of sailing you can think of.

Position 'in the fleet of 10' – 1st place if you are doing that aspect to Topper World Champion level. 10th place if you are doing it as well as an inexperienced club racer.

Importance – 10 points if it is crucial (starting, say) 1 point if it's useful but unimportant (e.g. gybing in 8 knots on the sea).

Result 'in the fleet of 100' – is the multiplication of the two scores out of 10. Pretty poor at starting – 7th place x 10 points = 70 points. Hopeless at gybing in 8 knots 10th place x 1 point 10 points. Clearly you will want to tackle the one with the highest score. That way you are maximising your training time.

How to improve at a particular aspect – this could be common sense but it may well be best to work this out with your coach.

Let's say you decide the starting problem is associated with not being able to hold your boat still on the line. Go out and practise. Find a fixed mark and play around it until you can control your boat in any conditions close to the mark without moving.

Perhaps it's a boatspeed problem and for this you need a friend. Sail close to each other until one boat is clearly ahead. Look at the settings on the faster boat and change the slower one to suit. When both boats are at the same speed then the real gains can be made. Make a change to one boat and see the effect: if it's faster change the other to suit, if it's slower then try something else.

Mental rehearsal

Sometimes it is difficult to get on the water and another technique becomes useful. Mental rehearsal is where you run through an action in your mind, from memory.

- Imagine a start in a big fleet. Try to experience it in the most realistic way you can and go though the sequence. The pressure should feel just like the real thing and you will get a little more used to it.
- Imagine a downwind leg in 15 knots and a great wave pattern. Feel the wave lift the back of the boat. Rehearse pumping the sail, imagine your body movements, feel the increase in speed and look ahead for the wave pattern, which will allow you to hop onto the next wave.

Physical preparation

Top sailors are physically very fit. If you aspire to Olympic sailing you will want to grow the body you will need in ten years time! Fitness gained in youth is important. This does not mean you have to go to the gym each day as Olympic sailors do, but it does mean the following:

- Eating healthily. There is plenty of information on diet especially on the use of complex carbohydrates to sustain performance over a long event. One useful trick is to eat carbohydrate within the first hour of finishing any physical activity; your body is keen at that stage to replace lost energy.
- Drinking plenty of fluid especially during physical sessions. A 2% drop in body fluid has been found to affect performance by 20%. Plain water will go straight through the system so a hydrating fluid is better. The easy solution (if you'll excuse the pun!) is a drink of 1/3 fruit juice, 2/3 water and a pinch of salt. If you feel lethargic at the end of a race ask yourself if you drank enough.
- Sleeping well, especially leading up to an event.
- Warming up cold muscles before you leap in a boat and blast off from the shore. Even before you lift a boat off the roof of the car and strain cold muscles! A very gentle 5-minute jog followed by stretching is the minimum. Don't stretch

The National Squad warm up.

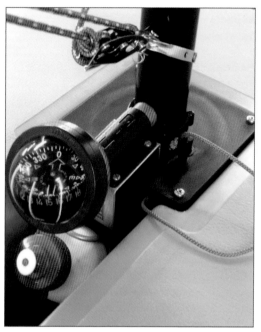

Site the drinks bottle here.

before the jog or you will damage yourself. Do this on arrival and then jog to the boat to re-warm before you go afloat. The added benefit is increased brain activity, which is useful in a sport that requires a lot of important decisions to be made.

- Warming down. Having worked so hard, a warm down jog is needed too. Remember, if you're not doing this and your competitor is then there will come a day when you are injured whilst he/she is not and then who has the last laugh!
- Read *Mental and Physical Fitness for Sailing*, also published by Fernhurst.

STORAGE

This is a big issue for Topper sailors. It has always been tricky stowing stuff in the boat so what can you do?

Fluids

Traditionally a bottle cage is strapped to the front of the mast but it's too high,

Storage bag for spares and food.

Fit the bag like this.

has large windage and is difficult to get at easily. This compass bracket can incorporate a bottle holder. It is easy to get to, low down and out of the wind. The bottle holds 700 cc but this is not enough fluid for back-to-back races. An additional bottle can be attached to a thin bungee cord that is secured to the boat. Pull the cord to drink, release to stow.

Food
Some kind of storage bag is useful, like the one in the photo. Sandwiches will get soggy so put them in a plastic bag as well. Clearly, these bags will be useful for spares too.

In the support boat
Three litres of fluid for three back-to-back races, each lasting one hour, would be difficult to handle. A support boat should be provided so that you can stow additional supplies. These kegs are big enough to

A water bottle and dry keg for spares in the support boat.

hold additional spares and an extra item of clothing.

The trick here is not to go over the top but be sensible and be prepared. Will you need to protect against the sun or a sudden cold patch? Food and drink matter, cost very little compared to the cost of big events, and have a big effect.

Final thoughts on you - and do remember that you are the most important part of any particular performance – not your boat, not your parents, not your coach, not your friends. It's you that matters, it's you that has to want to compete and above all it's you that has to enjoy yourself. This is not to belittle what the support structure, like parents, do for you. Far from it, they need to be appreciated and even thanked occasionally!

It's worth knowing what elite athletes are like. Research has looked at the best in a whole range of sports and it was discovered that elite athletes are:

FIT

MENTALLY TOUGH

DETERMINED

DEDICATED

SKILFUL – AT SAILING
SKILFUL - AT COMPETING

GOOD AT SETTING GOALS

HONEST WITH THEMSELVES

ABLE TO WORK FOR 10,000 HOURS

PEOPLE WHO RECOGNISE THAT
THE PAST DOSEN'T MATTER

Masterclass 2 Preparing your boat for success

Finding the right boat

There are over 40,000 Toppers out there somewhere so finding one should not be too difficult. Finding a boat suitable for racing is more of an issue. All the Toppers ever made have come out of the same mould so they should all be the same and they are pretty well indestructible.

Alternatively look for a boat used as a race boat and it will come with race controls and be well looked after.

Perhaps the best boats are ones left in a boat park for years and years. The grass may be growing around them but a quick power-wash and they will look (almost) as good as new.

What to look out for

Check that the mast cup, at the base of the mast, is not worn through and that the transom plate bolts can be fully tightened. Make sure the spars are straight and the sail has some service left in it. All spares are available and there is not a lot to go wrong in truth. Hulls and decks can be welded and leaks can always be stopped.

Check that the hull is not too scratched or distorted.

Maintenance is straightforward and a little time spent brings a lot of rewards:
- Tighten all screws but be careful not to overtighten.
- Clean the hull with bathroom cleaner and a plastic scouring pad. Deep scratches can be improved with 'wet and dry' glass-paper.
- Hose down with fresh water if sailing on the sea to slow down corrosion and to maintain the performance of the moving parts.
- The rivets on the mast and boom are stainless steel or monel. Check and, if necessary, replace them regularly.
- If water is getting into the watertight hull check the following by pumping the boat up a little (lung pressure will do) and applying washing up liquid and water to:

1. The self-bailer. This is best removed and re-bedded with Sikaflex or silicon sealant. There is a gasket between the deck and the hull in this area that can also be replaced with Sikaflex.
2. The transom plate. The captive nut on the inside plate can become detached preventing the bolts being tightened. Replacement of this nut is difficult (but not impossible) because hatches are not allowed under class rules.
3. The mast cup at the foot of the mast has a bolt that pulls the hull and deck together. This cup should be replaced occasionally to prevent damage to the deck as it wears away. Behind it there is also a seal that may need replacing. The bung should be sealed and possibly replaced.

4. The seal at the top of the plate case. Sikaflex and the use of negative pressure in the hull, using a vacuum cleaner, will cure this!

It is very rare to find that the deck-to-hull seal leaks.

HULL – Toppers are made of polypropylene and this must be taken into account. They are often miss-treated by non-racers because they are so difficult to destroy! Racers need to take special care. Hulls must be stored upside down or they take on a 'set' (wavy hulls are not fast!). Scratches are difficult to remove from the hull and oh so easy to put in! You can scrape them out but I prefer using 'wet and dry', starting with a rough grade and finishing off with 1000 grade and plenty of water. A good quality trolley that supports the hull in the right places is essential. A high handle position on the trolley will save your back as well as the transom of the boat.

DAGGERBOARD – Topper daggerboards are pretty well indestructible and not a bad hydrodynamic shape. However they are rather a sloppy fit. So:

1. Remove the hull plate and then the all-important daggerboard mouldings (bladders).
2. Clean up the inside surfaces of the daggerboard mouldings.
3. Attach Pro-grip to both of these surfaces – self-adhesive is best but if this is not available glue it with a contact adhesive.
4. Feather the edge of the Pro-grip with glasspaper or a file.

The daggerboard will now be a much tighter fit and has two additional advantages
1. It prevents the vertical scars found on almost all used daggerboards.
2. The daggerboard stays in the raised position without too much tension on the retaining elastic.

RUDDER and STEERING GEAR
The steering gear, as standard, is really sloppy so tighten and pack out as best you can.

I must say if you are going to spend time smoothing any part of your boat then do it to the rudder and daggerboard. They are under more pressure than the hull and much more inclined to stall out. You can spend the best part of a day 'wet and drying' a set of foils!

FOIL PREPARATION
Rudder blades and daggerboards really matter. Badly-prepared foils will adversely affect a boat's performance far more than the hull (although the very back of a boat has a pretty big effect).

In an ideal world foils should be stiff, light and a perfect aerofoil shape with a nicely-shaped elliptical front, an even curve that flattens out towards the back and finishes in a squared-off trailing edge perhaps 2 mm wide. Topper foils will never be ideal but then we have all got the same foil so it doesn't really matter.

You are allowed to 'repair' foils and you should spend a lot of time on them:

- Reproduce the shape of the bottom of both foils if they have been damaged. This may include the use of a blade acting as a scraper, file and rough glasspaper followed by ever-decreasing grades of wet and dry paper until it is very smooth.
- Check the front edges are chip-free and as elliptical as they were first intended.
- Smooth out any damage on the sides by using abrasive paper wrapped around a long flat piece of wood – thick MDF is great. Finish with 1200 grade wet and dry with lots of soapy water to wash away the particles being removed.
- On no account round off the back edge. As produced it is already too rounded.

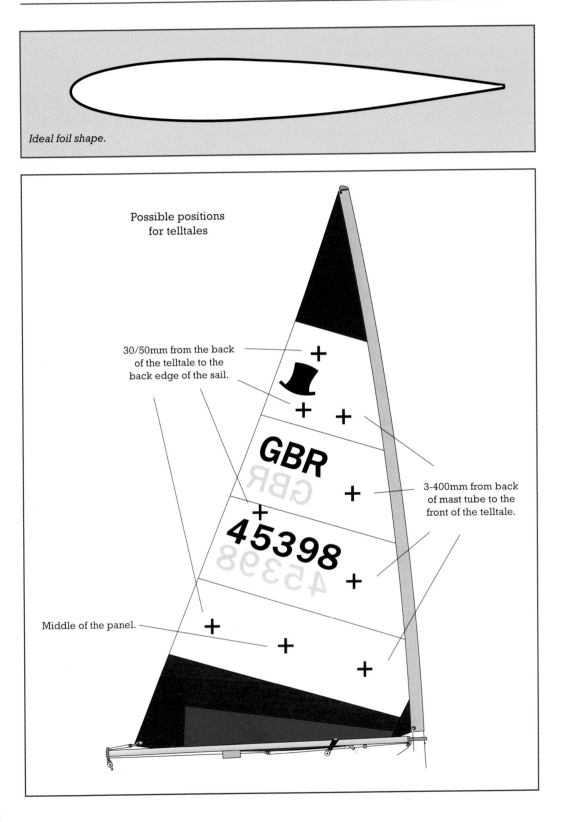

Ideal foil shape.

Possible positions
for telltales

30/50mm from the back
of the telltale to the
back edge of the sail.

3-400mm from back
of mast tube to the
front of the telltale.

GBR

45398

Middle of the panel.

- It is often necessary to smooth the moulding marks on the sides of the daggerboard. Fill with an epoxy filler and sand off.

This 'perfect' shape is impossible to achieve but at least you know what to aim for!

Of the two foils the rudder blade is more important. It is more likely to stall out because it is asked to work through bigger angles when the boat is being steered. A perfect shape diminishes stalling.

SPARS – The spars are generally good, especially the anodised ones.

The upper mast should be packed out with tape so it is a tight fit into the lower mast. This makes the mast bend as evenly as possible. Check and replace the rivets regularly.

MAIN HALYARD – Replace with a non-stretch rope and rig a 2-1 loop near the halyard cleat, or better still use a halyard loop.

AFT MAINSHEET SYSTEM – Ball bearing blocks and auto-ratchets are great here but much more important is that the mainsheet is at least 10 m long so the boom will extend beyond 90 degrees for that essential running by the lee technique downwind. Smart sailors have a knot in the rope so when the boom is at the optimum angle, and they are in the right position in the boat, the knot is in their hand. Rope as thin as 7 mm is used to allow the system to run smoothly

OTHER TRICKS – Like all simple boats that are being pushed beyond their original intended use, their helms have a thousand little tricks to make them work better as a race boat. Use the following as a checklist.

HULL

Rinse regularly, especially the mast cup. Clean with bathroom cleaner and (if necessary) a plastic scourer.

Bed down the hull plate by removing the top of the inserts.

Tape the join between hull plate and hull with parcel tape.

Tape the head of the mast cup screw.

Check the positioning of the foam block in the rear tank.

Check all screws for tightness but don't overtighten.

Centre toestrap held up with elastic front and back.

Side straps as short as possible.

Surf wax the sidedecks to provide grip.

Store the hull upside down.

FOILS

Clean regularly.

Smooth with wet and dry, especially the front edge.

Maintain a sharp squared-off back edge.

Tighten bolts on tiller and rudder stock.

Tape the top pintle to remove slack.

Progrip the daggerboard bladders.

Take daggerboard elastic to the front of the boat.

Aluminium/carbon tiller extension of maximum length.

RIG

Wash all fittings and fastenings regularly.

Check the boom and mast straps for loose rivets .

Check the lower mast for cracks around the strap.

Pack out the upper mast with parcel tape to achieve a tight fit.

Provide a backup rope for the mast strap and outer boom end fitting.

Velcro clew tiedown strap.

Sail stored by rolling around a tube.

Additional telltales attached.

CONTROLS

3:1 kicker with fiddle block and cleat.

6:1 downhaul with pull from forward.

4:1 outhaul with pull from forward.

2:1 traveller using dyneema or 'Spec 12' and roller clamcleat.

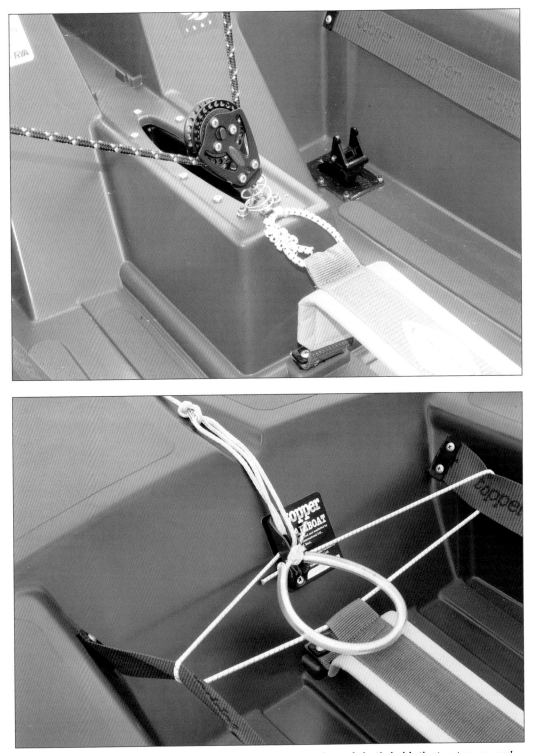

The front of the toestrap is held up by elastic. At the back one piece of elastic holds the toestrap up and the sidestraps in.

2:1 halyard using dyneema or halyard loop.
7 mm mainsheet 10 m length (or 12.5 m
for the centre main).
Handles or loops on control ropes.
Rope lengths adjusted to minimum.
Measurement strip on boom for outhaul
and mast for downhaul.
Measurement marks on kicker rope.
Dry lube mast to allow sail to move easily.
Dry lube controls for ease of use.
Dry lube boom to allow slide to move
easily.

OTHER
Compass.
Burgee and/or wind indicator.
Drinks bottle.
Bag for spares and food.

TOESTRAPS
The outer toestraps should be as tight as
possible to keep them out of the way.

Pad the centre straps for comfort and
grip. 'Kiwi – style' is good because it
prevents the padding rotating. Use elastic
to hold up this toestrap – the elastic at the
front is shown opposite. At the back, loop
the elastic around the outer straps and
under the centre one.

TILLER EXTENSION
Use the longest tiller extension that the
class rules allow - 975 mm - and use the new
rubber universal joint that won't lock up.

SOME THOUGHTS ON THE NEW 5.3 SAIL
The new sail is different:
- It has a more even depth throughout its
  height to give the leech better support.

So the leech flutters less - a bit of flutter
is OK but shaking is not!
- The deepest part of the sail is further
  forward to stop the boat luffing up into the
  wind when it really blows – with the old
  sail you inevitably finished up in irons.
- The downside of this is that in lighter
  winds the fullness at the front of the sail
  can reduce pointing ability. The solution
  is to pull on lots of kicker (vang) when
  sailing upwind even in light winds. This
  bends the mast and takes the fullness out
  of the front of the sail (it's much the same
  with the Laser Radial by the way). You
  can also pull on more outhaul to flatten
  the sail in light winds.
- The leech is cut with more of a hollow
  (take a look up the leech from clew
  to head) to minimise leech flutter.
  Another advantage is that you can now
  adjust the leech line without leech curl.
  Play with the leech line: let it right off in
  light winds and pull on in a breeze until
  the flutter stops. (The way to loosen it is
  to pull the leech tight with mainsheet or
  kicker and then release the line through
  the cleat.)
- Because of the stiffness built into the sail,
  don't allow it to flog between races.
- If the foot flaps, try tightening the foot line.

And one final point about the mast. With
the new halyard loop, when the downhaul
is loosened off downwind the two halves
of the mast can jump apart and pinch the
sail in between.
- File the ends of the mast tube.
- Keep the two halves from coming apart
  by taping them or use an off-cut from an
  old bike inner tube.

Masterclass 3
Advanced
control lines

You will need better ropes and more purchase if you want to race successfully.

WORLDS kit 2006	Dia (mm)	Type	Length (m)	Colour
aft mainsheet	7	Polylite	10	black or blue
centre mainsheet	7	Polylite	12.5	black or blue
outhaul front	4	Dyneema	0.45	blue
outhaul middle	4	Dyneema	2.1	blue
outhaul back	3	Pure Dyneema	2.2	blue
6:1 downhaul top	4	Dyneema	0.8	yellow
downhaul bottom	4	Dyneema	1.6	yellow
kicker	5	Dyneema	2.25	red
traveller	4	Pure Dyneema	3.25	yellow
halyard	4	Dyneema	6.5	blue/green
halyard loop	4	Pure Dyneema	0.75	blue

RACE	Dia (mm)	Type	Length (m)	Colour
aft mainsheet	8	Polyester	10	white/blue
centre mainsheet	8	Polyester	12.5	white/blue
outhaul front	4	Polyester	2.1	blue
outhaul back	4	Polyester	2	blue
3:1 downhaul top	4	Polyester	0.4	yellow
downhaul bottom	4	Polyester	1.6	yellow
kicker	5	Polyester	2.25	red
traveller	4	Dyneema	3.25	yellow
halyard	4	Dyneema	6.5	blue/green

STANDARD	Dia (mm)	Type	Length (m)	Colour
aft mainsheet	8	Polyester	9.5	white/blue
outhaul	4	Polyester	4	blue
1:1 downhaul	4	Polyester	1	yellow / orange
kicker	5	Polyester	2.5	red
traveller	5	Polyester	2.5	red
halyard	4	Polyester	6.5	blue
painter	6	Polyester	2	yellow / blue

MISC.	Dia (mm)	Type	Length (m)	Colour
centre strap	50	webbing	0.95	blue
outer straps	50	webbing	1.27	blue
front strap elastic	6	shock cord	0.4	white / red
back strap elastic	4	shock cord	1	white / red
daggerboard elastic	6	shock cord	0.6	white / red
d.board elastic to front	6	shock cord	1.5	white / red
PVC tubing for handles	8 ID	PVC tubing	0.33	clear

SHEET HORSE (traveller)

This is often overlooked but it is essential that the traveller is very tight in all but the lightest of conditions, so that the mainsheet blocks stay on the corner of the boat when going upwind and that the blocks do not come together before the mast has been bent by a sufficient amount.

Choose non-stretch rope such as 4 or 5 mm Dyneema. Replace the plastic clam cleat with an aluminium roller version to prevent slippage.

Make a purchase as shown in the photo and diagram: class rules allow a 2:1 system. Use a rounded (forged) shackle between the bottom mainsheet block and the traveller so that it slides better. Only decrease the traveller tension if the shackle won't cross the tiller in light winds.

The traveller on a top-end race boat.

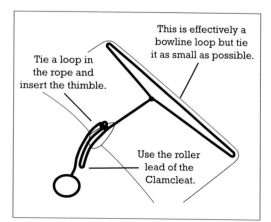

This is effectively a bowline loop but tie it as small as possible.

Tie a loop in the rope and insert the thimble.

Use the roller lead of the Clamcleat.

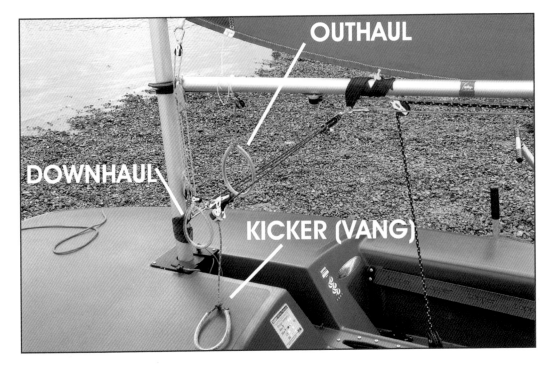

KICKING STRAP (VANG)

The original 2:1 'v cleat' system needs upgrading and a 3:1 with a fiddle block is universally used. Set the kicker at its minimum tension and then adjust the rope length so the handle is at the cleat. That way it becomes much easier to use your legs to apply the required force. You will have to push down on the boom in order to attach the kicking strap to the mast.

Pull in the mainsheet so that the blocks are 150 mm apart and take up the slack in the kicking strap. Now make marks, in line, on

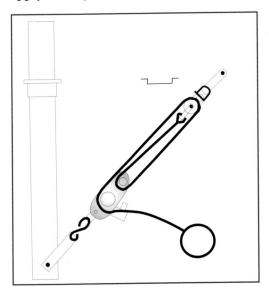

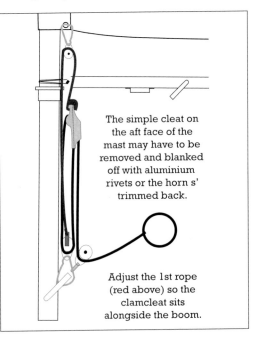

The simple cleat on the aft face of the mast may have to be removed and blanked off with aluminium rivets or the horn s' trimmed back.

Adjust the 1st rope (red above) so the clamcleat sits alongside the boom.

all three ropes. This gives a good reference for setting the kicking strap tension.

DOWNHAUL

Use a trapeze clamcleat arrangement with a turning block on the mast. Pull the handle, and the rope self-cleats. To release the tension, simply pull the rope out of the cleat. I must say that bigger sailors use less down-haul, it's the lighter sailor with a well-used sail who benefit most from this control. Pull on the tension upwind to bring the fullness forward and to decrease the power in the rig. Lubricating the mast will allow the sail to return to its original position when the control is let off for downwind legs.

HALYARD

If you use the old-style halyard there is no point in having an effective downhaul if the halyard stretches. 4 mm Dyneema is an excellent choice of rope. Form a loop in the rope as it exits the sail sleeve so a 2:1 mechanical advantage is obtained.
A bobble at the head keeps the sail, and therefore the boom, nice and high.

Better still use a halyard loop

Please note that the upper mast has been turned so the crane faces forward.
1. Feed the halyard loop up through the front hole in the mast crane.
2. Down the back hole.
3. Through the eyelets of the sail and back up the back hole (which might need enlarging slightly with a drill).
4. Loop the end over the bobble at the front.
5. So that it tucks under the bobble.
6 & 7. Pull the rope both sides of the crane and up into the groove on top of the mast-crane. This will tension the rope and so lift the sail.

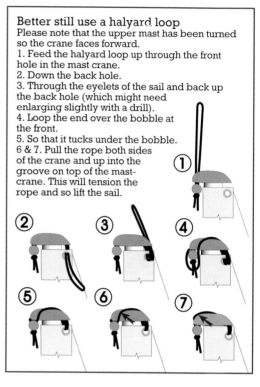

OUTHAUL

A 4:1 system is allowed and the one in the diagram works well. Replace the 'V cleat' with a camcleat and add a turning block at the mast. Tie a loop in the free end as a grab handle.

Note that there is a hook on the first part of the system that needs to be released when reefing.

The outhaul controls the fullness in the bottom of the sail. It really is hard to see the depth of your sail when sitting in the boat so apply measurement strips by one of the blocks to replicate fast settings.

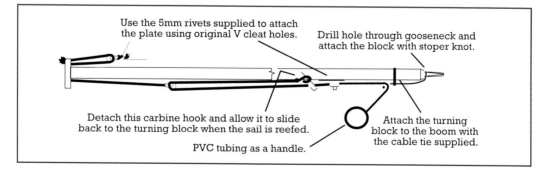

Use the 5mm rivets supplied to attach the plate using original V cleat holes.

Drill hole through gooseneck and attach the block with stoper knot.

Detach this carbine hook and allow it to slide back to the turning block when the sail is reefed.

Attach the turning block to the boom with the cable tie supplied.

PVC tubing as a handle.

Masterclass 4
Boatspeed and boat handling for success

The principle here is that you should work with the elements rather than against them.

1. HEELING ON A BEAT

The illustration shows the sort of sailing that is the opposite of what we're after.

The wind is strong and the sailor is fighting the elements. The boat is heeled despite the sailor breaking their back trying to keep the boat upright.

Because it's heeled the boat wants to round up into the wind (the curved side of the boat causes this). The sailor is pulling hard on the tiller to keep the boat travelling in a straight line and therefore the rudder blade acts like a brake because it's across the water flow. The wind is sliding out of the top of the sail, which de-powers the rig, but the boat is slipping sideways because the daggerboard is angled. To make matters worse the wind is getting under the hull and pushing it over and the weight of the mast and sail is acting against the weight of the sailor.

All the sailor needs to do is let out the sail! The boat comes upright and all these negatives disappear. Sailors tell me they are too light but if you are light you don't need the same power to go as fast as the heavyweights. It's about technique.

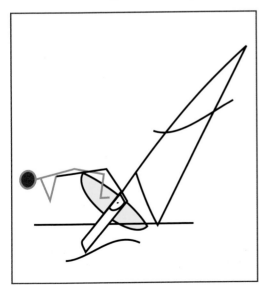

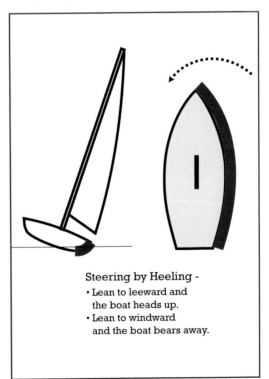

Steering by Heeling -
• Lean to leeward and
  the boat heads up.
• Lean to windward
  and the boat bears away.

The Enemy!

2. STEERING BY HEELING

When you are learning to sail, your rudder is your friend. When you start to race think of it as your enemy. Use it as little as possible and you maintain your speed.

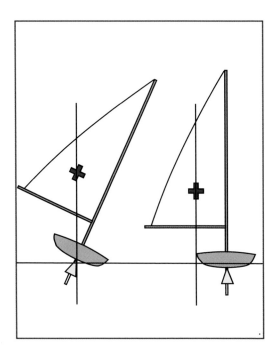

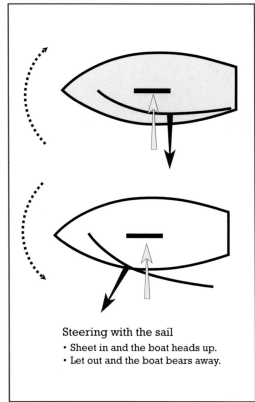

Steering with the sail
- Sheet in and the boat heads up.
- Let out and the boat bears away.

3. HEELING ON A RUN

Single sail boats should be heeled to windward when running. If they are sailed upright the point of effort on the sail spins them to windward and the helm will have to steer with the rudder to keep the boat tracking in a straight line. Heeling brings the point of effort directly over the point of pivot (the daggerboard) and the boat maintains a straight line without using 'the enemy'. There are two added advantages to this:

- The amount of contact between the hull and the water is decreased and that reduces friction.
- The sail is raised into the air where the wind is less disturbed and a little faster.

Once your boat is prepared and has controls that work you need to know how to use them.

4. DEPOWERING/ POWEREING UP

Flatten the sail

Easy really, a deep sail will give you power whereas a flat sail will give you less power. Lighter sailors will have to use all their strength to pull the controls on hard enough to flatten the sail. Fit the best controls you can, get the rope lengths just right and use your leg muscles to pull them on.

The principle – use the kicker, mainsheet and downhaul to bend the mast. A bent mast pulls the sail material forward which has the effect of flattening the camber in the sail, thus reducing the power.

The mainsheet – pulls down the back of the sail, which bends the mast by pulling on the tip. Be prepared to let the sail out if the boat heels. If the tiller extension is up your nose you are almost certainly heeling too much, trying to bear away when the heeled side of the boat is trying to make it head up.

The kicker – does the same as the mainsheet. In addition it drives the boom into the mast, which bends it. It also keeps the mast bent when the mainsheet has to be let out in gusts; otherwise when the mainsheet is let out the sail would become fuller which is bad news!

The downhaul – acts like a bowstring. It pulls the top of the mast down without pulling on the back of the sail. This makes it especially effective because the wind can escape more easily when the back of the sail is not pulled tight. Importantly, as well, it pulls the fullness in the sail further towards the mast, which counteracts the wind's effect of taking the fullness further back.

The outhaul – makes the bottom of the sail fuller or less full. It will also need to be pulled tight but don't overdo it or the sail will be too flat and have little forward drive.

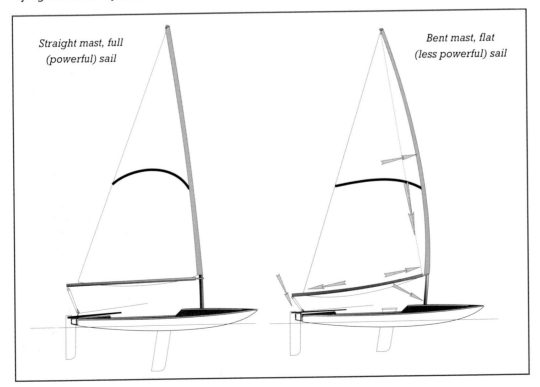

Straight mast, full (powerful) sail

Bent mast, flat (less powerful) sail

5. OTHER TIPS FOR WINDY CONDITIONS

Lift the daggerboard about 150 mm when beating; it will take the harshness out of the boat. Conversely, leaving a little more down when on a run will steady the boat by damping the roll. Remember to tighten the daggerboard elastic to save the board dropping out of the slot if you do turtle. (This is important.)

Give yourself more time and space to make manoeuvres. KISS (Keep It Simple Sunshine) is a great tip at all times but especially in a blow.

Keep looking towards the direction the wind is coming from so that you are ready to react before the gusts arrive rather than a split second later when it's already too late.

On a reach be prepared to bear away with the gusts (stronger wind) and try to come up in the lulls (lighter wind).

On a run sit well back and if you are still nose-diving put on more kicking strap (vang). Pulling the sail in more will steady the boat down but will make it slower (not as slow as upside-down of course!). Bearing away and sailing by the lee also reduces nose diving.

In flat water you can decrease the power on the beat by pinching higher than you would normally. You can feel the boat heel towards you as you overdo it. Weave a tight course that just keeps the boat flat when you are hiking hard. This will not work in waves because you need more speed to punch through them.

Upwind in waves be prepared to allow the boat to heel a little so the water slides off the deck before it arrives in the cockpit.

On the reach sit further back and keep the boat very flat.

When gybing just go for it – the faster you go into it the better chance you've got of coming out upright! Don't turn too sharply though.

Wear hiking shorts but make sure they fit correctly.

Tacking

Toppers, like a lot of single-handed boats, are difficult to tack in very strong wind. A few tips:

- Be bold. Go into the tack with plenty of speed (you may want to crack off a little as you approach the tack).
- Roll the boat over on top of you as you begin the tack.
- Cross the boat very fast, easing the sheet.
- Land on the new side and hike hard to bring the boat flat (or even heeled to windward), sitting as far forward as you can.
- If there are waves aim to be starting the tack as you go up the face of the wave. You will then be tacking at the top of the wave when both ends of the boat are out the water and speeding down the wave when you need to go faster.

If you do get stuck 'in irons' raise the daggerboard, sit further back, ease the kicker and let the sail out. Tease the sail in and as you start to move forward push the tiller away slowly and whip it back really hard. Repeat the latter several times to keep the boat off the wind.

6. REALLY LIGHT WINDS

In strong winds you need to be physical and do expect it to hurt – why should you feel different from everyone else! It's different in light winds. Imagine a cat, the way it stalks – complete concentration and total control. Still and ready to pounce into action when the time is right. This is just the way to sail in light winds. You can let the boat take you around the racecourse but it will be a lot faster if you are proactive.

The wind is always lazy, looking for the easiest route to follow but this is even truer as the wind speed decreases. It is not happy to travel around a deep sail and the merest jolt will knock it off course. These things help:

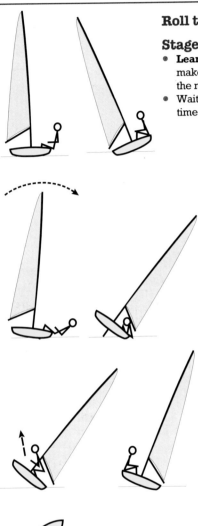

Roll tacking

Stage 1 – Initiating the tack
- **Lean into** the boat and sheet in more than usual. This will make the boat want to tack itself. In a two-sail boat sheet the main more than the jib.
- Wait until the boat approaches head to wind, by which time it is slowing down. **Wait longer than you think!**

Stage 2 – The middle bit
- Throw yourself out to the old windward side. This pulls the sail through the wind and gives you a pump just as the boat needs extra speed.
- The main will come across. Once it has, let out the mainsheet a little.
- **Wait** until the sail is on the new leeward side (it should be behind your head). You are still on what will become the new leeward side. The boat will be right on top of you (very scary!).

Stage 3 – Coming out of the tack
- Come across the boat (by standing up!) to the new windward side. Hike out no further than you were doing on the old windward side.
- As you move back across bring the main back to the position it was on the old tack.
- Pull the boat up slowly (the second pump) and powerfully but leave extra heel for the fiddle factor.

Use the 'fiddle factor' to correct the new direction of travel – if you need to luff allow the heel of the boat to head you up. If you need to bear off (which will have slowed you down) pull the boat upright, to increase speed, as you bear away.

Use as little rudder as possible
Use the extra push of the two pumps to spend as much time as possible heading towards the wind rather than speeding up, because coming out of a tack faster than going in is not allowed. A long curve through the wind is what is needed.

The grey boat is the finishing position of a roll tack that is too sharp a turn. The rule says you cannot exit a tack faster than you go into it. Use the extra push from two rolls to move further to windward rather than breaking the rule by coming out faster.

As I said this is difficult to describe but keep trying. I won an Open Meeting once, not because I was the best sailor but because I was the best roll tacker. We had to beat up a narrow river in light wind. The only way to make progress was to tack up the banks out of the current. In three races we did about 650 rolltacks. (We counted them in the last race and worked it out.)

Heel the boat so gravity is pulling the sail into the right shape. Heeling the boat also decreases the wetted surface area and so lowers friction.

- A boat down by the stern will drag its transom, which slows it a lot. Try sitting well forward and see how much better it goes.
- Move carefully but be prepared to spring into action when you need to – like in a roll-tack for instance.

7. ROLL TACKING

This is a complex subject and one that is best described by demonstration rather than words and diagrams. It is, though, an important skill to master. Think of a roll tack as a three-stage process: entry, process and exit (see diagram).

To begin with, your tacks will be worse, but do keep trying. Expect to get wet lots of times!!! In some boats all this happens without using the rudder (the enemy of speed) but in boats like Toppers you will have to use some.

8. ADJUSTING THE SAIL

The principles
In light winds a flat sail is needed. Achieve this with a tight(ish) outhaul. Do not use downhaul.

In medium winds it is best to have a full sail, achieved by using no downhaul, only a little kicker/vang and by having the outhaul at its loosest setting.

In strong winds it is best to have a flat sail, again achieved by using lots of downhaul and lots of kicker/vang but keeping some shape in the bottom of the sail with the outhaul.

Very little wind – below force 2
Kicker – sheet in the mainsheet so the mainsheet blocks are 200 mm apart. Take up the slack on the kicker.
Downhaul – none.
Outhaul – tight but not so tight that there is a crease in the foot of the sail.

Traveller – tight but just loose enough that the shackle can slide across the tiller without catching.

Hunting for maximum power – force 2 – 4
Kicker – sheet in the mainsheet so the mainsheet blocks are 75 mm apart. Take up the slack on the kicker plus a little more.
Downhaul – none.
Outhaul – so there is a maximum distance from the boom to the sail of about your finger length.
Traveller – very tight.

Overpowered – force 5 and above
Kicker – as much as you can pull on
Downhaul – as much as you can pull on
Outhaul – maintain the curvature of the sail.
Traveller – very tight.

These are a guide only. Much depends on your experience, weight and strength.

Settings
The settings in the table overleaf are in more detail but are also offered in th eright spirit. You cannot sail by numbers. Develop your sense of speed and adjust controls around these suggested start points

Note that settings on a reach are some-where between the Upwind and Running settings depending on wind speed and direction. For a close reach or when reaching in high winds, set up the controls nearer the Upwind settings. For a broad reach or when reaching in light winds, set up the controls nearer the Running settings.

Many experienced helms talk about getting feedback from the tiller extension. Grip it loosely and it will tell you things. Make a change to a setting and feel the effect.

9. ON THE WATER JUDGES – AND RULE 42

All sports need rules. In fact without rules there is no sport. What rig would you

Medium winds and flat water: (hiking fully but not overpowered)

Control	Upwind	Running
Mainsheet	Almost block to block	90+ Run by lee - in gusts bear away
Traveller	As tight as possible	As tight as possible
Kicker	Take up slack + a little more	Less – leech just able to flick
Outhaul	Sail a finger length from boom	Hand length from boom
Downhaul	Off or very little	Off
Daggerboard	Down	$3/4$ up
Balance	Flat	Heeled to windward - neutral helm
Trim	As far forward as possible	As far forward as possible

Medium winds and waves: (waves tending to upset the boat upwind)

Control	Upwind	Running
Mainsheet	Almost block to block	90 degrees – play the waves
Traveller	As tight as possible	As tight as possible
Kicker	Take up slack + a little	Less – leech just able to flick
Outhaul	Looser than flat water	Slightly tighter than on flat water
Downhaul	Take out some of the creases	Off
Daggerboard	Down	$1/2$ to $3/4$ up
Balance	Slight heel to leeward	Heeled to windward - neutral helm
Trim	250 mm further back	Forward and back - ride the waves

Looking for more power

Control	Upwind	Running
Mainsheet	300 mm off block to block	90+ and by the lee
Traveller	As tight as possible	As tight as possible
Kicker	Take up the slack	Less - until leach starts to flick
Outhaul	Width of wrist from boom	Length of hand
Downhaul	Slack	Off
Daggerboard	Down	$1/2$ to $3/4$ up
Balance	Very slightly heeled to leeward	Heeled to windward - neutral helm
Trim	Forward	Forward - stern out of water

Overpowered: (fully hiking and having to let out mainsheet upwind)

Control	Upwind	Running
Mainsheet	Block to block – let off	As far out as you dare. 80 deg. max
Traveller	As tight as possible	As tight as possible
Kicker	Take up slack + lots more!	As much off as you feel safe with!
Outhaul	Width of wrist from boom	Hand length from boom
Downhaul	Loads-until front stops backing	Off
Daggerboard	$1/4$ up	$1/2$ up
Balance	Flat	Heeled to windward - neutral helm
Trim	250 mm further back	Well back- prevent nosedive

choose to put on your Topper if the rules didn't limit you to the one we use?

The main difference between sailing and most other sports is that we are asked to police the rules ourselves. Boats are only measured at major events and on-the-water rules is policed by the sailors on the racecourse. This is why doing turns is so important and why I would encourage you to protest any sailor who breaks the rules. Protesting shouldn't be seen as an emotional business and the outcome should be accepted by both parties with a shaking of hands – we all need an inspirational goal!

Looking for any power at all! (very little wind)

Control	Upwind	Running
Mainsheet	300 mm off block to block	90+ and by the lee
Traveller	Tight – but allow block to travel	Tight – but allow block to travel
Kicker	Take up the slack	Less - until leach starts to flick
Outhaul	Reasonably tight - finger length	Reasonably tight - finger length
Downhaul	Off	Off
Daggerboard	Down	$1/2$ to $3/4$ up
Balance	Heeled to reduce wetted area	Well heeled to leeward
Trim	Far forward	Sit on bulkhead

The alternative is that we allow the cheats to gain advantage which none of us want.

What do judges look like?

Clearly, on the water judges are on the water! They will be in a RIB flying a yellow flag but be warned, just because you can't see them doesn't mean they are not watching you! You will also see them at the briefing where they will be letting the sailors know what they are looking for.

What are they looking for?

Principally they are looking for sailors who break Rule 42, which is all about illegal propulsion. You can read the cold facts in the ISAF rule book or even better go to the ISAF website where they will sell you a copy of the Rule 42 video at less than £5. On it is a series of clips showing legal and illegal propulsion and a written interpretation document. I expect that most clubs will be getting a copy soon so all learner racers start the sport better prepared.

42.1 Basic Rule

Except when permitted in rule 42.3 or 45, a boat shall compete by using only the wind and water to increase, maintain or decrease her speed. Her crew may adjust the trim of sails and hull, and perform other acts of seamanship, but shall not otherwise move their bodies to propel the boat.

Sailing is about... well sailing! It's not about air rowing and those who body pump, fan, scull, and pump inappropriately

need to join another sport. Governed by IARF rather than by ISAF no doubt! Actually windsurfers are allowed to air row!

It would take too long to set out in this section exactly what is allowed (sailing) and what is not allowed (air rowing) but here is a taste:

Sailing (allowed)

- Roll tacking and gybing
- Adjusting the sail when the boat changes direction.
- Moving your body weight in or out to help steer the boat.
- Using the rudder to steer the boat.
- Moving the mast over the vertical at the completion of a tack or a gybe.
- Torquing (upper body movement) to change the fore-and-aft trim of the boat in phase with the waves, provided it does not result in pumping the sails, especially flicking the leech.

Air rowing and other illegal propulsion (not allowed)

- Coming out of a roll tack or roll gybe faster than you went into it.
- Repeated tacks or gybes unrelated to wind changes or tactical considerations.
- Pumping the sail (rapid movement) except to promote planing (once per wave or gust and even then you must succeed in planing)
- Any sculling (two or more similar movements of the rudder, however small) that does not result in a clear change of direction (especially once beyond close

hauled when the sail can fill).
- Violent body movements like ooching (sudden forward body movement, stopped abruptly).
- Paddling! This includes any part of the body and movement of the boat in any direction (you can't stop by putting your hand in the water, for instance).

The above is only a taste and you would be best to read the rules, the interpretation of the rules (from the ISAF video), watch the video and talk to coaches and umpires.

The above should not stop sailors being active in a boat. I think of it as being 'on your toes' and you can tell a talented sailor by the attitude that sees them constantly checking their settings, looking around and changing their position in a boat as the situation demands. They are far more proactive rather than being reactive. The latter often results in over-exaggerated movement, which will be penalized.

Three pointers
- When you watch a fleet all the boats are being moved by the waves, unless it is very calm, at much the same frequency. The boat that is not being moved in the same way as the rest is clearly doing something wrong.
- Judges will look closely at the leech of the sail. If it is flicking (opening and closing repeatedly), irrespective of any action by the sailor, then clearly something is wrong.
- When boats are lining up for a start, and therefore manoeuvring at slow speeds, the temptation to scull is high. It may surprise you how little movement judges will allow. Sculling is the most penalised crime of all.

What happens if I break Rule 42?
The judge will let you know that you have broken the rule by blowing a whistle and pointing a yellow flag at you. Don't argue. Having spent a day with Carol Haines at the Inlands I know she was watching some sailors over a period of time and from a fair distance. By the time we motored up they were being very good (so they knew!) but it was already too late.

The first time you are caught at the event you must do a two turns penalty promptly (and without sculling or coming out of the manoeuvre faster than you went in or you will be penalised again!).

The second time (and this may be another race at the same event) you have to retire from that race (and if you don't retire you will be disqualified and have to count the result towards you final score).

If you are daft enough to do it a third time you will be disqualified from the whole event. This has happened at the Topper Worlds in the past, by the way.

This is pretty fierce stuff. Judges don't want to penalize you but they are there to see fair play so we are going to have to learn how to stay within the rules.

How can I get it right?
Ask! Coaches can help but the most important source of knowledge is the judge. They will hang around on the water between races and are keen to talk to sailors about what they did wrong and why they were yellow flagged. Even if you didn't get penalized and want to check a technique they will be happy to help – use them. Equally they are there after racing has finished and are very approachable.

10. A FEW MORE TIPS!
- *Sheeting in quickly.*
  Sheeting in quickly is especially important at the start but also at the leeward mark. With the centre sheeting, start by reaching down to the ratchet block with your front hand (the one not holding the tiller extension), then grab the rope and pull until your hand is over your head. Drop the rope carefully into the boat at the same time as you hinge the extension down and pick up the rope with your back hand.

Hinge the extension upwards (the trick here is to do this without steering in the wrong direction!) to allow you to pull the rope as you reach down with the front hand for the next pull. I often see sailors with a lap full of rope because they didn't place it carefully after a pull!

- *Responding to a sudden lift.*
  In a sudden lift you want to turn quickly into the new wind but it is impossible to turn that fast. Instead let out the mainsheet quickly (so that the sail is trimmed to the new wind). Then pull in the mainsheet again as you luff smoothly up to the new wind direction. The boat will spurt forward.

- *Beating – another technique.*
  Earlier in this book we taught you to beat by luffing until the front of the sail begins to flap, then bearing away until it stops flapping. A more subtle way is to sail by heel.

A. Get 'on the wind' and sit out (hike) so that the boat is almost flat. The exact angle of heel will be determined by the conditions, but you shouldn't have much weather helm.

B. Now luff gently whilst sitting out (hiking) the same amount. Eventually the boat will roll on top of you.

C. Now bear away until you are sailing at the same heel as in step A.

Keep repeating this technique and you will find that you can sail the ideal upwind course (without continually watching the sail) but instead taking in all that is happening around you.

11. THE FINAL WORD

Improving boatspeed and developing boat handling will improve results in small fleets. Practise them until they become second nature. Make them so automatic that even in stressful situations you still do things the right way. Even more important, make them so automatic that you don't have to think about them. When that happens you can concentrate much more on the bigger picture – on what other boats are doing and which is the best way to go. This is what will give you good results in big fleets.

Keep the boat upright like this, by hiking hard. Pull in the mainsheet until the blocks are close together.

Excellent beating. Sit well forward
unless the waves are breaking over the foredeck

Masterclass 5
Tactics and strategy
for success

Before the start
A boat race begins long before the start sequence. Time on the water, long before the first sound signal, will affect your result. Top sailors have a routine and so should you. The following is offered as a possible framework because preparation in this stressed period is very individual.

- On arrival take a look at the conditions and compare them with the forecast you already have. Check the geography of the land: will it affect the wind on the racecourse?
- Get on the first rank ashore so your launch times are not controlled by others.
- Launch early.
- As you sail out be observant of wind and tide. Has the race team set the course?
- Sail the first beat against a friend and see which side, if any, is favoured.
- This is a good time to set up the boat for the conditions.
- Determine the headings on your compass and see if the windshifts are oscillating or if there is a windbend.
- Windbends are best checked as you sail back downwind to the start area.
- Once the line is set, check the bias and take a transit.
- Work with your friend or coach to determine your tactics and strategy.
- Keep focused and warmed up as you recheck conditions up the course and the position of the line.

Starting
Once you can race a boat reasonably well the ability to start is probably the most important thing to get right. So how can you improve your chances of making a good one?

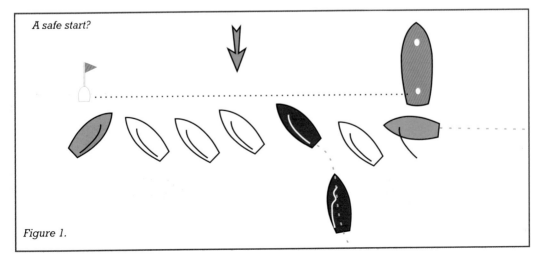

A safe start?

Figure 1.

A SAFE START

If you are inexperienced and a little nervous about starting, especially in big fleets, try this:

The rules say that the red boat (Fig. 1) can luff up as far as head to wind as long as it gives the boat to windward room to keep clear. Approach the line slowly and try to create a space to leeward. The grey boat reaching in at speed is about to remove everyone's wind indictors and the grey boat on port is also in trouble!

WHERE ON THE LINE?

Well certainly on the line, there is no point in being two lengths behind it or going the wrong way at the start signal! You will know, though, that the choice of position on the line can give you an advantage. The Race Officer will usually try to set a line that just favours the port end to counteract the advantage of being on starboard tack. If he/she doesn't make the

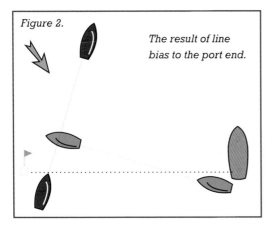

Figure 2.

The result of line bias to the port end.

port end 'biased' all the boats start by the committee boat – nightmare! However the wind rarely behaves so you need to check.

HOW CAN YOU TELL WHICH END IS BIASED?

There are a number of ways.

1. Reach along the line, or its extension, using your previously determined transits (Fig. 3). Let out the sail until half of it is lifting. Keeping the mainsheet in the same position, tack or gybe and sail the line in the reverse direction. If the sail is now flapping more you are heading towards the upwind end. If it is flapping less you are sailing away from the windward end. This is the best method for determining the upwind end when the bias is only slight.

2. The yellow boat in the diagram has luffed head to wind. With the sail flapping along the centreline your bow is pointing towards the upwind end of the line.

3. Get a friend to do a dummy start at one end of the line while you try the other (Fig. 2) . The one who passes ahead of the other has come from the upwind end.

BIG FLEETS

In big fleets with long lines watch out for 'line sag'.

Close to each end sailors can tell they are on the line. Further away from the ends it's more difficult to tell, so boats tend to play

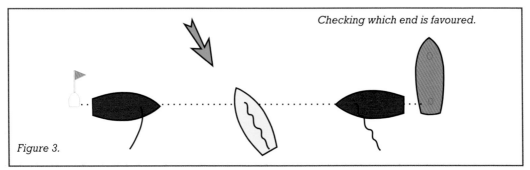

Checking which end is favoured.

Figure 3.

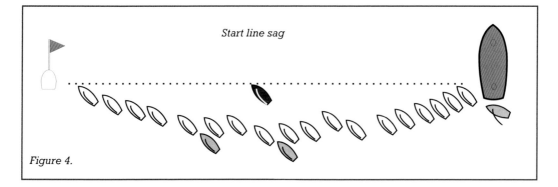

Start line sag

Figure 4.

safe, especially if it's a 'black flag' start. The smart sailor knows where the line really is and you can imagine the advantage gained and the cries that come from the rest of the fleet when they believe you are over the line! The grey boats are still being donkeys!

Remember to consider which side of the beat you want to play. Even if the line is port biased, if you want to go right up the beat, starting at the port end may be a bad idea.

PLOTTING THE LINE
If only the Race Committee would paint the line on the water! But they don't so how can the black boat tell? What you need is a transit. Look along the line (from outside either end) and find a fixed feature that lines up (Figure 5).

Sometimes there are no transits visible. Try this alternative, the 'tiller method': When you think you are on the line point the bow of the boat at one end and centralise the tiller. Look along the tiller (still centralised) and, if you are on the line, it will be pointing at the other end. If you are behind the line (often the case!) the tiller will be pointing behind the line. If you are over the line it will be pointing ahead of the other end. It is remarkable how often you think that you are over the line when you are not.

OTHER IMPORTANT POINTS
- Allow for the current.
- Also, you still need to have a reliable stop-watch and know how to use it and trust it! Particularly on long lines when you are at

the opposite end from the committee boat, start when your watch tells you and not wait until the sound signal reaches you.
- Good boat control is essential. You must be able to speed up and slow down, manoeuvre in tight corners and have a good idea how long it takes to cover a particular distance in a particular time.

TOP TIPS FOR FIRST BEATS!!!

- Know the settings that give you boatspeed in particular conditions.
- Have a plan based on wind and tide but be prepared to change it. One way of checking this is to sail the first beat, before the start, against a friend who goes another way. Don't miss the start though!

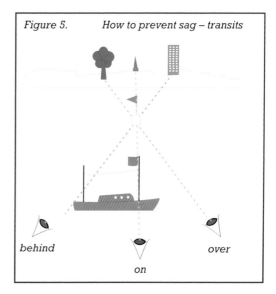

Figure 5.   *How to prevent sag – transits*

behind   *over*

on

- Get a good start. Very bad start? – go across the back of the fleet on port until you find clear wind. The wind you get as you cross behind the fleet on port, although 'dirty', is lifted.
- Clear air, clear air, clear air..........
- First 100 m go for boatspeed – keep your lane.
- WORK VERY HARD ON THE FIRST BEAT!!!!
- Look out for the first windshift. Be far enough ahead to use it. WINDSHIFTS REALLY COUNT!
- When ahead stay between the bulk of the fleet and the first mark.
- Be prepared to duck boats – sail your own race.
- Get your head out of the boat.
- Don't go to either layline. Work the side

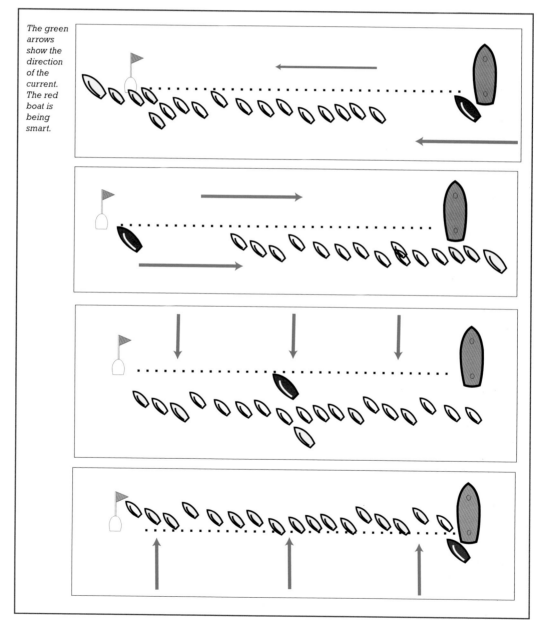

The green arrows show the direction of the current. The red boat is being smart.

of the beat that suits your plan.
- If you believe the right side is the better side (perhaps there is more wind) and the fleet goes left then only be more to the right than most of the fleet, i.e. be conservative.
- Check your plan by coming back to the sweet spot – the middle (ish).
- In general in a big fleet the best advice is to come into the first mark on starboard.
- But don't hit the starboard layline too early.
- Think ahead to your strategy on the next leg.

Windshifts

On a beat of 200 m two boats set off from the leeward mark. One goes on a 9-degree lift while the other goes the other way on a 9-degree header. Halfway up they both tack just as a windshift happens. The one on the lift gets another 9-degree lift whilst his unlucky competitor once again gets the 9-degree header. By the windward mark the first boat has a 100 m lead!

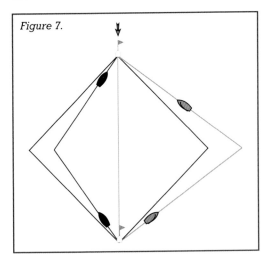

Figure 7.

The orange boat is the unlucky one who catches two bad 9-degree headers while the blue boat gets two 9-degree lifts. The black tracks are what would happen if there were no windshifts.

This shows the importance of windshifts and, while you would be very unlucky to be

as badly out of phase with wind as the orange boat, 9 degrees is half of one division on a tactical compass!

No amount of boatspeed will make up for being on the wrong side of a bad windshift, so how do we recognise them?
- Look at other boats. Those further to windward than you will get the wind change first and you can be ready to react. Boats in line with you will appear to go backwards when you are on a lift and appear to go forward of you when you are on a header.
- Your boat will slow down and stop heeling as you encounter a header. In a lifting wind you will be able to head up without the boat slowing.
- In a header your sail will back in a big shift but before that the telltale on the windward side of the sail will drop.
- Your wind indicator will change direction.
- Above all, your compass will show a change in your heading.

COMPASS

Compasses are useful all round the racecourse but especially on the beat. They are really easy to use. Buy a tactical compass and it will have numbers on it. Sail on each tack for a while and you will find the magic number. If it is 12 on starboard then it will be 2 on port. They are always 10 apart – 4/14, 8/18 and so on. Write this number on your boat. When the number goes up on starboard you are on a header. On port the number goes down when you are being headed. Draw a minus sign on the port side of the boat and a plus sign on the starboard side. Sail your boat and when you feel you are on a header take a look at the compass as confirmation of the fact – don't sail looking at it all the time!

Types of windshift

Oscillating – The wind shifts either side of its average position. The timescale for the shifts is often consistent and can be tracked by sailing upwind while making a note of when the shifts happen. Remember though that when going downwind the shifts will be further apart because you are travelling with rather than against the wind. In oscillating winds it's best to sail a little freer when you are on a lift so you get to the next lift (on the other tack) more quickly.

Windbend – wind will often follow the contours of the area it travels in. If it bends, always tack towards the inside of the bend.

Permanent shift – where the gradient breeze is gradually shifting one way, head towards the side of the beat it is swinging to. If it's swinging to the right, that will be the favoured side of the beat.

Offwind

Tactics offwind are a little less complicated. Clearly you must keep clear air and everyone else wants to do the same. One effect of this is that there is often a large bow and few boats take the direct route to the mark. This can be exaggerated where tide has an effect. On broader reaches, on longer legs and in bigger fleets look for the option of going low immediately you exit the mark and staying low until you approach the next mark. There are big gains to be made here. But how do you know that you are on the direct line to the

next mark? Look again at the way you can get a transit for the startline and use the same technique for offwind legs. As you round the first mark, look over the next mark at a feature beyond. Keep the two in line and you are on a straight-line course. Sometimes you will have to crab sideways to keep the two in line but that will indicate the presence of a current.

In Figure 8 the fleet is behaving like sheep – a fleet often does! The grey boat is in the worst possible position, in the fleet's dirty wind. The red boat has gone for clear air and will often gain lots of places.

Rounding the leeward mark

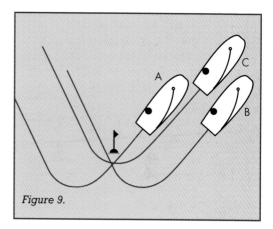

Figure 9.

Traditionally, we all round the leeward mark like boat A – wide in, tight out. This is good if you are in the company of lots of boats, because you are best placed to avoid too much bad air from those in front and at the same time prevent those behind you working up to weather and preventing you tacking.

However it is worth pointing out that, in the absence of other boats, B, rounding with the same radius turn as A, but coming in close and exiting wide gets an equally good result. i.e. is as far upwind as boat A after the rounding.

Amazingly, there is a more efficient way of rounding. C rounds so that the mid-point of her curve is the buoy, so

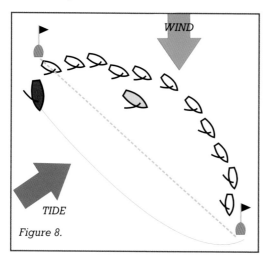

Figure 8.

she will have sailed the least distance downwind. However, this rounding should only be used when you're well clear of other competitors!

Top Ten Tactical Tips

Tactics is about boat-on-boat manoeuvres, whereas strategy is about dealing with the elements – if there were no one else in the race what would be the fastest way around the course?

This list of tips came from a smart group of junior sailors who were limited to only the ten they considered the most useful – the ones to fall back on when all else fails!

1. Maintain clear air.
2. Keep your head out the boat.
3. Don't be greedy – play the percentage game. Make little gains. Don't take risks.
4. BOGTOSS! – pre-start checks:
- B – Bias – check the line bias
- O – Observations – look around, especially for transits
- G – Gusts – what is the wind doing up the course?
- T – Tide – check the tidal flow
- O – Obstructions – for you to avoid and for the wind to flow around
- S – Shifts – what is the pattern of the shifts?
- S – Speed – Boat set up for the prevailing conditions
5. Long tack first – there has to be a good reason not to be taking the long tack first to the windward mark.
6. Land on the left go left – the wind tends to be stronger (but is it? Do check.).
7. Up on starboard, down on port – if you spend most time on starboard tack upwind you are likely to spend more time on port gybe coming downwind.
8. Get on the lifting tack as soon as possible – after the start or on rounding the leeward mark.
9. Get on the inside of an anticipated windbend.

Take control – sheep don't win boat races!

Tide on the course

Smart sailors make allowance for the tide. The grid on page 121 predicts what a 'STUPID' fleet would do in tidal flow A. Do the same for B, C and D.
Fleets are stupid, individuals are bright – get your head out of the boat.

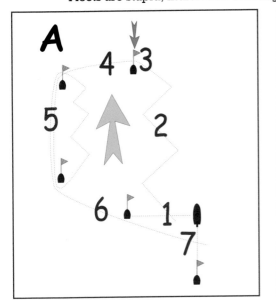

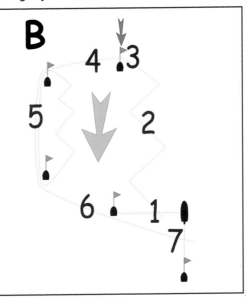

A

1	Start	The fleet will be over the line
2	Beats	There will be more waves than normal - wind against tide
3	Windward Mark	The fleet will overstand the laylines
4	Top Reach	There will be a big bow to windward
5	Run	Running downwind will be against the tide and so take longer
6	Bottom Reach	There will be a big bow to windward
7	Finish line	There will be lots of boats at the committee boat end

B

1	Start	
2	Beats	
3	Windward Mark	
4	Top Reach	
5	Run	
6	Bottom Reach	
7	Finish line	

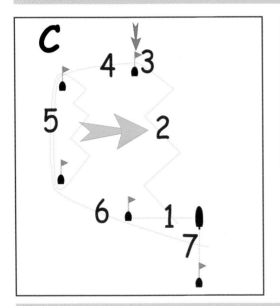
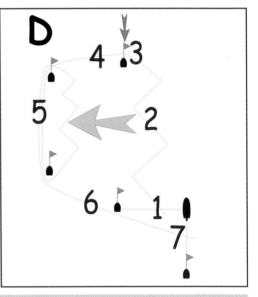

C

1	Start	
2	Beats	
3	Windward Mark	
4	Top Reach	
5	Run	
6	Bottom Reach	
7	Finish line	

D

1	Start	
2	Beats	
3	Windward Mark	
4	Top Reach	
5	Run	
6	Bottom Reach	
7	Finish line	

Masterclass 6 Preparing for an event

Competition is stressful. Sound organisation will prevent many stressful situations and increase the chances of a good result.

You may recognise the following
- Running out of time on the day so you arrive late at the start area.
- Forgetting your stopwatch and not having a spare.
- Finding the travel lodge didn't have your booking after all!
- Not having a spare boom end fitting when one breaks.
- Forgetting a towel in your sailing kit.

So get organised!

Months before
- Check the events you want to compete in.
- Book the accommodation and ferries.
- Make checklists for equipment, clothing (sailing and otherwise) and spares.
- Make a time plan and sequence for the day of the race.

Weeks before
- Download the Notice of Race and entry form.
- Enter.

Days before
- Read the sailing instructions and prepare any questions.
- Get the forecasts.
- Look at the charts and maps to relate the venue and likely wind directions.
- Download directions to the venue and determine travel time.
- Work back from the start time to determine what time you need to leave.

This is another case of 'Fail to Plan and you Plan to Fail'. You will know how naturally organised you are and therefore how detailed the lists need to be. The following spares list is based on my personal experience.

Spares list
On water:
- Length of 4 mm rope.
- Bung!
- Carbine hook.
- Traveller shackle - will do for other applications.
- Chinagraph pencil and rubber for writing info on the boat.
- Drink - hydration fluid is best.
- Food for immediately after the race, if not during the race.

Tool box:
Endless!!!
- 4 mm dyneema.
- 4 mm elastic.
- Knife and lighter.
- Various shackles and carbine hooks.
- Sif (old Jif) and rag to clean hull.
- S/S rivets and rivet gun (needs to be beefy - some groups buy one between them - Screwfix or Machine Mart).
- Self-bailer.
- waterproof tape - parcel or gaffer

- More bungs!!!
- Insignia cloth (same as used on sail numbers) for sail repair
- 10 mm spanners for steering gear
- Phillips screwdriver
- Mastgate lanyard.

One could go on! In truth the fleet is very friendly and will help out so some of the above is a bit OTT.

Masterclass 7 Dave Cockerill's guide for parents

What can racing do for your youngster?

Sailing is a brilliant sport. To succeed at sailing you need the kind of skills you need to be successful in life:

- Confidence - if nothing else the confidence gained by being responsible for your own actions and for a vessel in a hostile environment and most often coming back alive! There aren't even any roads to navigate on! Some parents are unlucky enough not to get on the water. If they only knew the things their child was going through at times!
- Planning skills – goal setting is a high level skill. Even looking ahead six months to decide what events to attend is an experience worth having.
- Making friends – you have to help each other in this sport. You have common experiences, often ones well worth reliving together (those waves were as big as bungalows!), and you go away together.
- Physical prowess – the open air if nothing else. Those who think that sailing is about fluffy white clouds, blue sky and pink gins have never tried sailing.
- Mental ability – toughness, making connections, seeing the bigger picture, assertiveness, playing a percentage game. It goes on and on. I'm often told that sailing has had a positive effect on an individual's schoolwork. Rarely have I heard the opposite despite the times homework is done in the back of a car on the way to an event.

The commitment

I have been a squaddie parent, following my son around and eventually racing a Topper myself because he was clearly having lots of fun. It all started in a small way – club race, local regatta and then local Open Meeting. You meet other parents; share a great experience or two and suddenly you're at the National Championships in some remote corner of the UK for your holidays. The funny thing is I found myself having fun and enjoying the progress he was making.

Here it gets tricky. There is a difference between enjoying your child's progress and living through him. One attitude supports what they are doing willingly, the other expects results from what you have done. The worst thing I ever heard was a child who was scared to go ashore at a windy event because "Dad will shout at me". I nearly resigned that day as National Coach because I felt the parent's attitude stemmed from the seriousness of it all. A seriousness I thought I might be adding to. There is plenty of pressure on sailors to do well from within, from peer pressure, from wanting to do well for coaches and yes for wanting to do well for parents. Too much pressure diminishes performance. As a coach I try to remove pressure. Looking at the long view is important. How good were they twelve months ago? How good will they be in twelve months time? Less pressure means better results and more fun.

Fun

Fun is the most important thing. It is pointless coaching a sailor who is not having fun. All that effort will be wasted if they don't enjoy sailing, because they will move on to other activities. We lose too many great young people to the sport because they are put under too much pressure. It's a sport for life, not just for teenagers!

Support before and at the event

As your child gets older you will be able to extend the range of things they can do themselves. Involve them in the planning progress, expect them to prepare and rig their own boats but do be there to support their efforts. They are young and will make mistakes.

I quickly recognise (are you listening Adam?) that my son needed space when he came ashore. The last thing he needed was involving me in what happened in the race even though I was keen to share the experience. The stories might come out in the car on the way home, if he wasn't asleep! Certainly they would come out over the course of the next week. Despite

that he would never ask for my advice – what did I know? When I thought there were things he needed to know I would prime my brother or another parent who would make the suggestion on my behalf. Equally other parents primed me and it all worked very well.

Oddly enough I stopped watching through binoculars because his results seemed to get better when I didn't know what was going on!

Coaches

Coaches are great people! We love what we do but it can be stressful and help is welcomed. I like to have a parent in the coach boat with me. It makes me a far more effective support boat and I do need someone to lay marks! There are two rules however:

- only one voice should come out of a coach boat and that's from the coach.
- you must not mention your child (biologically impossible of course!)

If you decide to employ a coach and your youngster is already in a squad then it is a good move, as well as professional courtesy, to ask the extra coach to contact the squad coach who will know the areas the sailor needs to develop next.

And finally – silly games

Just in case this is all getting too serious...
   The best two non-sailing games have long-established rules.

CLIMBING THE MAST

1. Take all gear off the boat except the mast, daggerboard and (old) sail.
2. Wrap the sail tightly round the mast and tie it off.
3. Have two people stand chest deep in the water, one holding the bow and the other the transom.
4. Attempt to climb to the top of the mast before the boat falls over.
5. Prove your achievement with a photograph.

MAXIMUM NUMBER OF PEOPLE ON A TOPPER

The official record is 17 (see photo). This particular group in Dubai are sure they had 18 on the boat but I can only see 17 so 17 it is.

   Can you do better?

1. Remove all gear from someone else's Topper. (You wouldn't want to use yours would you!)
2. Put it in waist deep water.
3. Get as many people as possible on the boat.
4. The boat is allowed to go under water but not on the bottom (no cheating!).
5. The boat must be afloat for 10 seconds.
6. Prove your achievement with a photo!

OTHER GAMES

How many different ways can you capsize a Topper? Here's a start: The Pitchpole!

You rely on us.
Can we rely on you?

Become an Offshore member from just £5.00 per month.

Last year, our volunteers saved over 7,000 people. But we couldn't have saved a single one of them without the support of people like you. Join Offshore today, and you'll be helping to run the Lifeboat service whose volunteers will be on hand, should you ever get into difficulty at sea.

Call **0800 543210** today.
Or visit **www.rnli.org.uk**

Offshore

registered charity no 209603